PUBLICATIONS OF THE
BERNARD VAN LEER FOUNDATION

IMPROVING EDUCATION
FOR DISADVANTAGED
CHILDREN

Some Belgian Studies

Other titles in the Series

IMPROVING EDUCATION FOR DISADVANTAGED CHILDREN

Written for the Bernard van Leer Foundation
by *Service de Psychologie génétique de l'Université Libre de Bruxelles*

Laboratorium voor Ontwikkelingspsychologie van de Rijksuniversiteit Gent

Laboratoire de Pédagogie expérimentale de l'Université de l'Etat à Liège

Département des Etudes et des Recherches Psycho-pédagogiques de l'Université de l'Etat à Mons

BERNARD VAN LEER FOUNDATION
THE HAGUE

and
PERGAMON PRESS

Oxford · New York · Toronto
Sydney · Paris · Frankfurt

U.K.	Pergamon Press Ltd., Headington Hill Hall, Oxford OX3 0BW, England
U.S.A.	Pergamon Press Inc., Maxwell House, Fairview Park, Elmsford, New York 10523, U.S.A.
CANADA	Pergamon of Canada, Suite 104, 150 Consumers Road, Willowdale, Ontario M2J 1P9, Canada
AUSTRALIA	Pergamon Press (Aust.) Pty. Ltd., P.O. Box 544, Potts Point, N.S.W. 2011, Australia
FRANCE	Pergamon Press SARL, 24 rue des Ecoles, 75240 Paris, Cedex 05, France
FEDERAL REPUBLIC OF GERMANY	Pergamon Press GmbH, 6242 Kronberg-Taunus, Pferdstrasse 1, Federal Republic of Germany

First edition 1977 - De la Stimulation compensatoire à une Pédagogie rénovée/van stimulering tot Paedagogische vernieuwing, 1969-1975.

First English edition 1979

British Library Cataloguing in Publication Data

Improving education for disadvantaged children: some Belgian studies.
1. Socially handicapped children - Education (Preschool) - Belgium 2. Compensatory education - Belgium
I. Universite libre de Bruxelles. *Service de psychologie genetique* II. Bernard Van Leer Foundation
371.9'67   LC4096.B/   79-40036
ISBN 0-08-024265-0

In order to make this volume available as economically and as rapidly as possible the authors' typescripts have been reproduced in their original forms. This method unfortunately has its typographical limitations but it is hoped that they in no way distract the reader.

Printed and bound at William Clowes & Sons Limited Beccles and London

Contents

Note on the Bernard Van Leer Foundation

From its earliest beginnings as a philanthropic body concerned with supporting a range of humanitarian activities, the Bernard van Leer Foundation has had at the heart of all its actions the exploration of various ways whereby education can be seen as a means of realising man's inborn potential and the special relevance of this idea to the educational needs of the disadvantaged. The expression of this concept is necessarily dynamic and continuously changing.

In 1966 the Foundation became an operational institution and its subsequent interventions were based on the conscious choice to discover how, in conditions of adversity, educational innovation could contribute to individual and social development. In being responsive and responding to activities that contribute to the creation of the opportunities available to the deprived, the Foundation had to be prepared to take risks, investing its resources in experimental actions often beyond the capacities of the established authorities.

Over the years it has built up a core of professional experience and expertise and since the early seventies this has been increasingly brought to bear on its worldwide project network and where possible, enriching it and diversifying it. There is now a trend in the direct interventions by the Foundation towards involvement in projects with major national bodies whereby it is expected that a formative influence can be exercised on a policy and planning level to bring the special requirements of the disadvantaged within the purview of general educational provision.

In its continuing concern with early childhood education, the Foundation acts in accord with the directions indicated by much current research; but equally it does not depend on the outcomes of such research to validate exploratory moves into new spheres of activity. By 1978 there is clear evidence of an increasing realisation that to consider the young child in isolation from his family and community does not make sense, if long-term educational gains are to be realised. A significant number of the Foundation's current projects are now active in helping the school to acknowledge the importance of parents as crucial partners in the education of their children; in making school and community more accessible and more responsible to each other; and in enabling communities through a variety of collaborations, to help others.

It is an important Foundation objective that the work of successful projects should be disseminated and replicated both nationally and internationally. This monograph exemplifies one aspect of the way in which the Foundation seeks to explore the fundamental problem of liberating the disadvantaged child from the restrictive pressures of a variety of constraining environments.

A Note to the English Edition

The action researches reported in summary form in this book, were conducted a few years ago (1969-1975) but the work has continued to act as an influential leaven in the Belgian school system. The studies are interesting not only because of their findings but because they represent the first attempt in a bilingual (French/Dutch) European country to examine problems which had been occupying research workers in the United States and Britain since the late 1950s.   Indeed their origin - and that of the corresponding Anglo-Saxon studies - is very much earlier than that.   Beginning with the work of Maria Montessori (an Italian) and of Decroly (a Belgian), 'compensatory education' in a variety of forms, has crossed and recrossed the Atlantic several times in the past decades.   They are too a part of a considerable series of studies of these problems supported by the Bernard van Leer Foundation in many countries, which over a decade or more and still now concern themselves with children in the vulnerable period of the pre- and primary school years.

What is characteristic and instructive about this Belgian research is that, instead of working in some sort of artificial experimental situation outside the normal school system, its activity has been firmly based within the schools and in the homes.   All action research in education tends to raise issues which go beyond any one of the sciences involved and to confront the research worker with ethical, moral and political issues, and the closer it comes to the daily reality of the classroom the more this is inescapably so.   It is moreover, to a degree difficult for the outsider to assess, dependent upon the assumptions which govern the day-to-day working of the particular educational system. Normally the most influential of these are inexplicit and enshrined in a tradition taken for granted. We become aware of this as we read work like the present.   Sometimes the differences from our own system are more apparent than real and lie rather in verbal formulations than in any difference in fundamental conceptions.   But often this is not so and structural and terminological similarities conceal profound differences of cultural style and expectations and consequential school climates.   These are likely to be reflected in all kinds of ways difficult to detect - in how teachers view themselves and their professional role, the relation of the teaching profession to the curriculum, the importance accorded to inspection, the attitudes and part played by parents, how educational administration relates to the schools and the place of educational policy in politics.

Glimpses of this will be found even by the casual reader of the following pages. A teacher from the United Kingdom, for example, would be somewhat startled to learn that a pupil in the primary school might be kept down to repeat a year's work.   He or she would be even more surprised by references to the 'programme' by which is meant a detailed curriculum to be covered in a school year, prescribed centrally by the Ministry of Education, and expected to be followed identically by all schools.   That such a prescriptive curriculum should extend even to pre-school education would seem even more strange.

Matters like these affect directly the autonomy of the teacher and of the head of the school to determine policy and curriculum within more or less wide guide-lines.   This has its counterpart in the attitudes of parents to the school and how they can hope to exert influence.   An American reader used to the power, involvement and activity of Parent-Teacher associations might find it difficult to believe that most Belgian schools keep parents at arms length, many parents rarely cross the threshold and then usually when their child is in some sort of trouble. A centralised and imposed curriculum also tends to define the role of the inspect-orate.   In countries like Belgium and France, inspectors are truly inspectorial in their function; in some less centralised systems, their tasks are those of administrative liaison and technical advice; their influence pervasive and persuasive rather than authoritarian; their activities concerned with consultancy and inservice training rather than with checking on how far teachers are teaching and pupils learning a prescribed body of material.

It is differences like these that make the very means and possibly even the content of innovation in education very different from one country or system to another.   Whereas the techniques of fundamental research in child development and psychology can largely be replicated in laboratories all over the world, particu-larly with very young children, transfer of the practical methodologies of action research in education would be dangerously simplistic.   Most of the work on compensating for disadvantage had been carried out in systems which were reasonably flexible and where the possibilities for change were not inhibited by rigid administrative regulation and structure.   Even so, by no means all of it has accepted the necessary constraint of working through the existing structures in order to change them if necessary.   It would be fair to say that - like other educational systems of Napoleonic origins - the Belgian school system is heavily centralised and highly structured.   It is resistant to change from below, as it were.   Within it even good and innovative teachers find no great room for manoeuvre. Beyond the small changes that any teacher can make in his personal style and in the presentation of standard material, innovation and the conditions fostering innovativeness have to be created or at least sanctioned by authority and supported from outside.   This apparent inflexibility is probably matched by the fears and expectations of at least some of the parents who know that in a system, progress through which is marked out in clearly defined paths, departures from the conventional may lead to apparently irretrievable disaster.   More open and less structured systems like those in some parts of the USA, Canada or England, may seem to provide more evident opportunities for teacher initiative, may seem to allow pupils to retrieve later on in their education any failures or wrong turnings they may have made (though this is far from certain in any system) and appear to be generally less selective, less ruthlessly élitist and more democratic.

This is probably an illusion.   Failure is failure to a child whether expressed overtly and administratively by grade repetition or by markedly inferior attainment in basic subjects in the primary school, which prepares for a more general and definitive failure at the secondary stage.   What is probably not an illusion - and experience in countries as diverse in their systems as Sweden, the United States and England seems to prove it - is that fundamental reform in education does not come about by legislative and administrative fiat, however centralised or decentralised the system.   It can only come about by changes from within, changes in attitudes and educational styles, in systems of relationships which govern the transactions between pupils and teachers, teachers and parents, and between these

and the educational administrators.   How this is to be achieved in detail, the
nuts and bolts of innovative change as it were, will be largely influenced by the
constraints and general climate of the educational system itself and the surrounding culture, particularly that of the family.   These will determine the overt
face of teacher and parent anxieties which are among the main obstacles to change.
The structures of the schools and the training of the teachers will determine how
innovation is to be created within and fed out to the educational system as a
whole.

It is in the glimpses of this process at work in a centralised and - as those
belonging to it believe - rigid and inflexible system that the richness of these
four cooperative projects resides.   The theoretical and practical findings are of
great interest and significance for the general theory of education and doubtless
of very positive value to the Belgian educational system.   But the student from
outside will be as interested as much if not more in the ways in which action
research, initiated in universities, accepted the constraints of an existing
system, worked successfully within them, and by shifting its centre of gravity
from the special experimental set up or laboratory to the field, opened up a real
dialogue among all the partners.

o   o
o

This work is a translation of "De la Stimulation Compensatoire à une Pédagogie
Rénovée - Van Stimulering tot Paedagogische Vernieuwing".   In this English version
certain sections, notably the thorough survey of the literature prepared by the
University of Ghent, have been omitted since they do not bear upon the situation
outside Belgium or can be found in other forms elsewhere.   On the other hand, an
additional chapter has been included in Part 2 and in Part 4, showing recent
developments in the field.

In order to make clear to the English or North American reader some of the
situations or basic concepts, it has been necessary here and there to depart from
a literally faithful translation and reformulate the issues raised.   It will be
noticed too that certain terms for pre-school institutions in the original French
or Dutch have not always been given their precise verbal equivalent: pre-school
has been used as the general term and 'nursery school', 'nursery' and sometimes
'pre-nursery school' have been used as the general context of the original text
suggested correspondence with the system generally in use in the United States and
Britain.   If as is possible these are still superficially misleading, the
surrounding context usually makes it quite clear what kind and stage of education
or child care is being referred to.

General Introduction

The four brief accounts included in the present volume present an overview of a Belgian inter-university project funded by the Bernard van Leer Foundation.

The teams associated with the project are: the Service de Psychologie génétique de l'Université Libre de Bruxelles (Department of Genetic Psychology of the Free University of Brussels, Professor P. Osterrieth); the Laboratorium voor Ontwikkelingspsychologie van de Rijksuniversiteit Gent (Department of Development-al Psychology of the State University of Ghent, Professor W. de Coster); the Laboratoire de Pédagogie expérimentale de l'Université de l'Etat à Liège (Depart-ment of Educational Research of the State University of Liège, Professor G. de Landsheere); the Département des Etudes et des Recherches Psycho-pédagogiques de l'Université de l'Etat à Mons (Department of Educational Studies and Research of the State University of Mons, Professor J. Burion).

An interim report was published in 1973 on the occasion of a colloquium held at Esneux (Belgium) and which had as theme: the diagnosis and the compensation of socio-cultural handicaps. At that time the research work was well under way. It is still not finished; the four teams are actively working further on this most crucial problem of education - but the inter-university project itself has ended.

The title of the present document published on the occasion of the Steenokkerzeel colloquium (March 1977) indicates a profound change. Its wording: "From compen-sation to innovation" shows how the research workers' approach has changed. From the initially relatively narrow notions both as to the children themselves and the contexts of their lives, their view has widened to embrace an examination of the whole of education. The chronological order in the presentation of each of the four reports documents this process of growth.

All men are not born with the same physical and mental potential. One will be tall and strong, while another, in spite of closely similar treatment, will remain small and weak. And for any particular task, one will be handicapped compared to the other - the handicap never being total nor invariably peculiar to this or that. A recognition of this simple fact bids us, without being naively egalitarian, to see to it that everyone has the chance to develop and to learn to his full capac-ity. This opportunity for full growth is not always there even in the similar environments, the family, the larger social groups, the school or the 'media'.

From this point of view, even when it is thought necessary to pay particular attention to one or another sub-population of children, one notices that the concept of compensating for socio-cultural handicap has to give way to a theory of individualised and constructive education.   Nor can action be limited to cognitive aspects; it must give equal place to socio-emotional development; and approach the problem not only through the individual but through the whole relational, organisational and institutional context of his life.

Abandoning symptomatic treatments and adopting a constructive approach based on individuals and their broad social contexts, the Belgian researchers have gone beyond the earlier concepts of compensatory education as a way of meeting deficits. Deliberately too they conducted their research in real contexts and worked in cooperation with all the partners of education, particularly parents and teachers. Hence the work of the Belgian project developed the conditions which specialists in innovation regard as the only efficient ones for a real change - research acting as a catalyst enabling the system and its participants themselves to generate the ideas and their embodiment in practice.

It is worth remarking too that the University teams themselves have changed. Although they started from very different positions, they have ended, as if by an inevitable process of development, with agreement on the general theory and philosophy of action and research.   At a time when universities are criticised for unwillingness to join together, it is worth underlining that, given the possibilities of cooperation and a common ideal, real inter-university cooperative structures can develop.   Now there is in Belgium a group of researchers used to working together, linked by mutual respect and well qualified by experience.   This is no mean source of satisfaction.   Although this was not its major objective, the intervention of the Bernard van Leer Foundation was decisive in this development.

In fact what the Bernard van Leer Foundation wished to do was to give primacy to pre-school education as a major area of educational research in Belgium, to develop a wider awareness of the roots of social inequality in education and to provoke a critical reappraisal of educational institutions.   This is what happened.

Eight years of reflection and intensive intervention in the field have thus borne fruit and raised hopes.   A conviction, well founded in the facts, that a step forward has been made towards the solution of a problem of major importance is the best reward for the research worker and the best encouragement to continue to work for the community.   But, at present it is not easy to be optimistic. Concern must be felt that current economic and political crises dramatically affect action research programmes aimed to reduce social inequality - as if cultural democracy were a luxury reserved for periods of abundance.   There is a real risk that, without a constructive and far-sighted policy, the present crisis will doubly affect the victims of the economic and social situation, by preventing the wide application of research such as this and by not enabling such enquiries to continue.

Part 1

Socio-cultural Handicaps in Early Childhood

Summary of the research undertaken by the Service de Psychologie génétique de l'Université Libre de Bruxelles.

Prof. Paul A. Osterrieth
Prof. Anne Cambier
Marie-Sygne Billen-Pohl
Ariane Bogaerts
Nicole Carels
Colette Deguent
Bernard Versele

Introduction

The term 'socio-cultural handicap' usually refers to a pattern of psychological characteristics supposedly common to a great number of children from socially and culturally deprived environments, which would make these otherwise physiologically 'normal' children more or less able to take advantage of the primary education available in all industrialised societies. This, in turn, would prejudice their full participation later on in the intellectual and cultural life of our times. In this way a state of inferior intellectual development and a process of socio-cultural marginalisation is built in.

It would seem to be a matter of fact that unadjustment to the conditions and requirements of school frequently becomes apparent at a very early stage, as soon as the child begins to go to school. According to many observers, this 'socio-cultural handicap' is noticeable even in the pre-school, where the demands placed on the child differ from those of the primary school. The fact that school or pre-school seem to lay bare or even accentuate interpersonal differences as soon as attendance begins, indicates that such differences are related to the original environment, and exist prior to the start of formal education. We are thus naturally led to think that if a 'socio-cultural handicap' does indeed exist, the factors responsible for it operate before the appearance of any sign of inferior intellectual development and of learning disability. Because of the complex nature of psychological development and behavioural organisation, it is to be expected that many of these factors will have little, if any, obvious or immediate connection with what is generally meant by intelligence and school aptitude. This fundamental hypothesis leads us to look carefully at the pre-school stages of a child's development. The period between 6 and 24 months is of particular interest: during this period the development of behavioural organisation is particularly rapid and the child is generally thought to be undergoing basic structuring experiences. This hypothesis prompts us to focus on the experiences offered to the young child and on the influences of the family and of the crèche, a substitute and nowadays increasingly complementary environment to that of many homes.

This type of approach seems likely to bring to light any psychologically meaningful variable, intermediate between the socio-economic or socio-cultural status of the family and the child's individual aptitude or capacity to profit subsequently from its schooling. It could help to throw light on the genesis and determinants of the phenomenon of failure - an obvious prerequisite to any preventive or compensatory action.

With this in mind we attempted, with a sample of children from a district of the Brussels area, to explore the possible relationship between:

- the socio-economic and cultural status of the families;
- the level of behavioural development of the children;
- the attitudes and behaviour of the parents towards the children.

At the same time, a psychologist familiar with the problems of early childhood was sent to a large crèche in the area.   His task was to identify the circumstances and factors which, in the crèche, were likely to cause underdevelopment in children; to suggest, in agreement with management and staff, appropriate measures to minimize or eradicate such factors; and to encourage any measure which might make the environment of the crèche more favourable to the development of the children. An account of this experiment can be found in Chapter 3 of the present report.

1 Population and Procedure

1. Sampling and Data Collection

Three hundred and fifty families, all with few exceptions living in the district of Anderlecht, were identified from an examination of the population register. In February 1973, these families were informed by letter that a research project was to be undertaken concerning the education of very young children; and were invited to collaborate. They were also told that they would soon be visited, to ask for their consent and to make an appointment for a further interview.

At the first meeting, the parents were informed in detail of the object of the research and of what was expected of them. This first interview also gave the opportunity to collect the following information, as a means of screening families for inclusion in the sample:

- full details of the mother's and father's occupation to give a more accurate evaluation of socio-economic status;

- a brief and rapid evaluation of the family's housing conditions;

- details of the child's birth history (term) and medical history (serious illnesses);

- the language of the home.

Another appointment was made if the parents had given their general agreement to being involved.

The second meeting was devoted to a largely unstructured interview with the mother at home and with the child present. This enabled us to observe the interactions between mother and child. The mother's responses were not specified by a direct questionnaire. She was simply asked to talk freely about her child and its education, and she was left completely free to broach any topic she liked. In the course of the interview (but without interrupting) some specific survey questions were slipped in. The interview lasted normally one hour, and was tape-recorded in full, which gave no problem. Finally, mother was handed a questionnaire. She was told of its purpose and shown how to fill it in. She was asked to complete it during the week between the second and third interview.

During the third interview and in the mother's presence the child was given a battery of developmental tests by a team of two psychologists. One, specially

trained to administer the test, presented the material to the child.   The second,
who had interviewed the mother on the previous occasion, observed and recorded
the child's behaviour.

At the same third interview, more precise information was gathered about the
socio-economic and socio-cultural levels of the family and the child's developmental history.   The questionnaire given at the preceding meeting was collected
when it had been filled in.   Generally, these visits took place in a friendly
atmosphere.   Many mothers seemed pleased at the opportunity to talk about their
child; some even asked for further visits.

The procedure was followed for all the 90 families retained in the sample, which
were then divided into 3 equal subsamples according to the three independent
variables: sex (46 girls and 44 boys), age of the children (30 children aged 10
months, 30 aged 15 and 30 aged 21 months) and the socio-economic status of the
family (30 families of lower status, 30 families of average status, 30 families
of higher status).   Other background information was taken into account, such as
birth data, serious illnesses, sibling order, separations from mother longer than
a fortnight, and so on.   But it was not possible to form strictly equivalent
groups on the basis of these additional background variables.

2. Assessment of Socio-economic and Socio-cultural Levels

It was of importance to define and assess socio-economic and cultural level if
we were to meet the preoccupations and objectives of the Bernard van Leer
Foundation.   Initially to carry out the interviewing and to set up our sample
of 90 families, we used the single index method, currently applied in this field.
The selection of the sample was thus based on a 'cumulative index' which took
into account occupation, educational level and physical aspects of the home.   It
very soon became clear that this cumulative criterion was too coarse and not
likely to take adequate account of many facets of so complex a concept as socio-
economic and cultural status.

Accordingly a second stage, during data processing, we decided to make a factor
analysis of the detailed information we had.   This allowed us to assess the
relative importance of a series of indices derived from our raw observations.
Nine indices, each carefully defined and assessed on a normalised 5-point scale
emerged as follows:

1) Highest occupational level (father or mother)
2) Father's education
3) Mother's education
4) Joint income
5) Appearance of the neighbourhood
6) Household equipment and help
7) Number of bedrooms per person
8) Number of living rooms per person
9) Standard of housing

This method made it possible to classify the sample in a more sensitive but still
objective way, on the basis of the scores for each of the three factors thrown
up by the factor analysis.

- The main factor which appeared can undoubtedly be interpreted as a socio-
  economic factor.   All nine indices used are saturated with it and are thus
  all related, to some extent, to socio-economic level.

- The second factor is related to living space in the home - the two indices
  most saturated in this factor being 'the number of bedrooms per person' and

'the number of living rooms per person'.

- The third factor largely accounts for the variables 'appearance of the neigh-bourhood' and 'standard of housing'. It corresponds to the 'outward signs of social success'.

These last two factors are of slight importance in comparison with the main one, and account only for a small proportion of the variance. Nevertheless, we continued to use them as they provide information complementary to the socio-economic factor.

A similar procedure was adopted for the following 24 indices on cultural matters:

1) Classics and modern novels
2) Political, historical, psychological, touristic, biographical books and periodicals; literary and art reviews; art books
3) Detective novels, romances and science fiction
4) Newspapers and weekly publications (Nouvel Observateur, Pourquoi pas, Express, etc.)
5) Fashion and home magazines (Femmes d'aujourd'hui, Libelle, Rosita, Bonnes soirées, etc.)
6) Glossy magazines (Jour de France, Match, Marie-Claire, Elle, etc.)
7) Classical music
8) Pop music and jazz
9) Theatres and concerts
10) Dances and balls
11) Engagement in a sport
12) Evenings with friends
13) Lectures - museums, exhibitions
14) Films chosen on the basis of their title or kind
15) Films chosen on the basis of reviews; favourite television programme
16) Documentaries and news
17) Films
18) Light entertainment
19) Favourite radio programme: music, concerts and light entertainment
20) Intellectual games
21) Games of chance
22) Hobby connected with the home: knitting, crochet, sewing, etc.
23) Cultural, artistic or aesthetic hobbies (playing an instrument, house decoration, reading)
24) Holidays abroad

A factor analysis of these indices also threw up three factors:

The main one corresponds to a rather traditional concept of the 'cultured man'. We find grouped together the lectures, the visits to museums and exhibitions, theatre going and attendance at concerts, the reading of classic and contemporary novels. This factor was named 'classical culture'.

The second factor appearing from the factor analysis was called 'popular culture'. It is represented by the following cultural indices: games of chance, watching films on television, dancing, reading detective novels, predilection for detective films, science fiction and westerns.

The third factor noted was called 'consumer culture'. It is characterised by holidays abroad, a predilection for pop music and jazz, reading glossy magazines and a preference for light entertainment programmes on television.

3. Assessment of the Child's Level of Development

For many reasons, the Brunet-Lézine (1) development test, similar to that of
Gesell, appeared to be the most suitable tool for this investigation.   The
Brunet-Lézine test explores four areas:

- postural-motor behaviour

- motor coordination, manipulation of objects

- verbal behaviour

- social behaviour

Results are expressed as a quotient of global development, based on total items
succeeded.   Four partial quotients of specific developmental aspects corresponding to the four behavioural areas mentioned above, can also be obtained.   The
quotient of global development allows an estimate of advance or retardation in
comparison with 'normal' development.   The partial quotients are useful to
determine whether, for example, retardation shown by the overall quotient is
general to all four areas or is due to low performance in one or more specific
area.

Analysis of the test, however, showed it to be not fully adequate to our research
needs and some improvements proved to be necessary.   A refinement of the methods
of administration and scoring made the test rather more reliable and improved its
sensitivity;   a standardised observation schedule was also added which enriched
the test score by qualitative data of the utmost importance;   classifying the
behavioural responses into 32 categories instead of the original four made it
possible to achieve a finer analysis of the child's level of development.   This
Brussels adaptation of the Brunet-Lézine test is a more efficient instrument,
which should prove useful in the examination of young children.

The variables which emerged from the information provided by the new version of
the test are the following:

- the 5 developmental quotients originally put forward by Brunet-Lézine (general,
   postural, coordination, verbal, social).   On these the subjects were grouped
   in three classes according to their score: below average, average and above
   average (respectively, 1/5, 3/5, 1/5 of the sample).

- 9 indices of development which allow subject to be ranked according to the
   level of their performance (the total of succeeded items in each of the
   following areas):

   - form discrimination (*)
   - comprehension of oral commands (*)
   - oral expression
   - object association
   - problem solving
   - coordination of the upper limbs
   - locomotion, sitting posture, gross motor coordination
   - reactivity
   - spatial organisation (*)

   The three areas marked with an asterisk (*) were applied in the 10 months old
   group; again on each of those developmental indices, subjects were divided
   into three groups (1/5; 3/5; 1/5).

- An index of harmony/disharmony in development.   This was based on the degree
   of homogeneity among the four partial quotients;   in this case subjects were

divided into two groups 'harmonious' - 'disharmonious' dichotomy.

- <u>5 indices of coherence</u>, reflecting for each of the developmental quotients the difference between the age at which all items are passed (the 'basal' age) and the age placing of the highest item passed. Each of these indices (in the spread) gives an idea of the cohesiveness of performance. For this, subjects were again dichotomized into 'coherent development' - 'incoherent development'.

4. Assessment of Parental Attitudes

Because of the great difficulty of making systematic observations of family life and studying the behaviour of both parents' behaviour towards the child over an adequate period of time, it seemed best to use a more practicable means of investigation: the non-directive interview. When parents relate incidents, events and anecdotes drawn from everyday life, they consciously and voluntarily provide a great deal of information on situations in which they are involved with their child. In addition, certain elements in their conversation give clues to fundamental attitudes, ways of behaving and deep feelings. These elements of a situation which parents remember and describe, the objective and subjective elements they include, the importance given to other's and to their own feelings, the very topics chosen, those which are discussed in detail and repeatedly alluded to, those only vaguely mentioned or passed over in silence, the choice of words, tones of voice and so on - all these are rich in content. In short, such a talk reflects both the way individuals view the circumstances consciously, their overt ideas and attitudes (the kind of material one hopes to tap by a questionnaire) and also the deep-seated structures of personality which are more subconscious and more deeply emotional (to tape which usually we use projective tests).

The non-directive or unstructured interview thus seems to be doubly useful: it only minimally constrains the subject's full expression, and it allows a form of expression which reveals both the deeper levels of feeling and social behaviours, attitudes and their underlying dynamics. It seemed that unconstrained and personal talk would be the best source of information on, or the best indicator of, the nature and climate of the adult-child relationship.

The real difficulty is that of extracting useful information from these records and organising it so that it can be extracted. For this purpose a content analysis, designed to elucidate psychological meanings and to isolate and define variables, was carried out by a team of five judges to ensure maximum reliability and validity. For the purposes of our research we focused only on those aspects bearing upon communication between parents and children and on relationships - 25 categories emerged which were grouped as follows:

a) 'training' variables
b) 'psychological proximity-perception' variables
c) 'contact' variables
d) anxiety indices
e) manifestations of feeling
f) areas of child behaviour most chosen for comment

There is an obvious difficulty in scoring these categories in a satisfactory way. Individual interviews of a non-structured kind cannot be directly compared one to another. Mothers did not utter the same number of sentences; some used less of the allocated time than others; sometimes other persons present at the interview (e.g. father, another child) intervened. This difficulty it appeared might to some extent be overcome if the frequency of appearance of each variable or group of variables were expressed as a ratio of the total of all variables appearing in the same conversation.

The 90 frequencies so obtained for each attitude-variable or group of variables were first ranked, and then grouped into three classes - below average (1/5), average (3/5), and above average (1/5).

5. The Questionnaire

The sources of information so far described have certain gaps: the tool used to assess development gives little information about the child's emotional reactions or sociability.   Similarly some particularly important attitudes of mother may not appear in the course of an interview and therefore be omitted from the analysis.   For example, the commonly held view that children from privileged environments are more stimulated in the field of spoken language than children from deprived ones made it seem interesting to gather information from all parents about whether they sometimes looked at picture books with their child. This kind of activity might be passed over in an interview.   To cover gaps like this, we constructed a questionnaire.

The variables which we finally attempted to tap with this questionnaire differ both in content (child's behaviour or parent's attitude) and in the way they are derived: some were covered by a simple part of a question, others by adding together different parts from a number of questions.

REFERENCE

(1) Brunet, O. and Lézine, I. Le développement psychologique de la petite enfance. P.U.F., Paris. 1965.

2 Results

In this research the significance of relations in the data was tested where possible by X^2, and only differences significant at P = .1 or better are mentioned. This obviously is only a first approach to the data.

It should be recalled too, when reading what follows, that any relations observed merely reflect the probability of two characteristics coexisting or not in different groups. It does not indicate necessarily a causal relationship, still less the direction of any causal connection there may be. We have thus to consider any relations or significant differences that appear in a multidimensional context, taking the findings about each in the light of the whole, by differentiating the effect of given variables.

1. Socio-economic and Socio-cultural Level of the Families and Level of Development of the Child

Is there a link, for all the age groups considered, between the socio-economic and socio-cultural status of the families and the level of general or specific development of the children? By relating the socio-economic and socio-cultural factors and the developmental variables it becomes possible to arrive at an answer to this question.

In view of the objective pursued, one essential feature emerges from this first comparison. Out of the 60 possible combinations between the 3 economic factors and the 20 developmental variables, only 3 links are found to be statistically significant:

- children from families with a low socio-economic status tend to be more advanced in the development of locomotion, sitting posture and general co-ordination.

- children from families with average living space show, more frequently than others, a superior quotient of general development.

- children from families with inferior living space tend to obtain better scores for the co-ordination quotient.

As there is a significant link between the living space and socio-economic status, the last two connections in no way support the hypothesis according to which material well-being fosters the child's development. In fact, they might suggest the opposite, since above average living space is associated with low quotients of general and of co-ordination development. As to the socio-cultural variables, there is no apparent link between them and the indices of development.

It seemed worthwhile to look at the question differently, by extending it beyond one-to-one connections between isolated variables. If one considers the children with at least 3 out of 5 developmental quotients in the above average group (15 of the 90 children) as 'more developed', and children with at least 3 developmental quotients in the below average group as 'less developed' (17 of the 90 children), we can then examine the distribution of these extreme cases in relation to the socio-economic variables (Table 1).

TABLE 1 Distribution of the Most and Least Developed Children
in relation to Socio-economic Variables

Development	Socio-economic Level	Living Space			Outward Signs of Social Success		
		Superior	Average	Inferior	Superior	Average	Inferior
15 Most	superior N=4	–	4	–	1	2	1
Developed	average N=4	1	2	1	1	2	1
Children	inferior N=7	1	5	1	3	2	2
N	15	2	11	2	5	6	4
17 Least	superior N=6	4	2	–	1	3	2
Developed	average N=7	2	1	4	4	2	1
Children	inferior N=4	1	1	2	2	2	–
N	17	7	4	6	7	7	3

Two important conclusions can be drawn from the table.

(i) Nearly twice as many children shown by the combined results of the tests to be advanced in their development come from deprived as compared to privileged environments. Over three times as many children who fall into the least developed group come from average or privileged environments.

(ii) Five times as many children exhibiting superior development come from families with average living space as from families either with above or with below average living space. Children exhibiting low development come three times less often from families with average living space than from families with above average or below average living space.

The combination of socio-economic level and living space seems thus related to the child's general development, at least in the extreme cases. The role of the factor 'outward signs of social success' seems to be ambiguous; the most we can say is that it seems very slightly but not significantly more important in the case of the families of the less developed children.

A similar analysis of the socio-cultural variables confirms that these have practically no bearing on the level of development.

To conclude, it would seem that for children 21 months or less of age, the economic status of the family has only an indirect link, if any, with the various aspects of development considered in isolation and that cultural status has no apparent link whatever with development, at least not until the child is 21 months old.   This does not, of course, rule out the possibility that socio-economic or cultural factors are already at work, but simply that their effects do not yet appear.

There is no indication in these data that children from deprived environments are necessarily handicapped in their initial psychological development, nor that children from more privileged environments exhibit superior initial development. This finding, if it is sustained, is of major importance for the study of 'socio-cultural handicap'.   It prompts us to believe that, if such a handicap indeed exists, it does not show in the first two years, and that, if there is an explanation for it, it is not at this moment to be found in the socio-economic and cultural conditions of the family in their strictest sense.   These conclusions lead us to think that the variables describing mother's attitudes are the ones which should be studied.

2.   Socio-economic and Socio-cultural Level of the Families and Mothers' attitudes

Attitudes of the mothers as revealed in the interviews may well be linked with the socio-economic or socio-cultural context.   The degree of material well-being, the richness of information and culture, the existence of family traditions favouring severity or gentleness, warmth or distance in affective relationships might well be among the factors contributing to shape these attitudes.

In fact, many relations emerged between the socio-economic and socio-cultural variables on the one hand and the attitude-variables on the other.   Twenty out of the 25 variables of attitude studied are significantly associated with economic or cultural variables, frequently indicating a marked difference between privileged and deprived environments.   Without going into details, the observed links and differences noted can be summed up as follows:

(i)   With regard to the socio-economic factor: more mothers from privileged environments are characterized by:

- emphasising training less,

- having greater psychological closeness to and better understanding of their child,

- a more marked propensity to express their feelings.

(ii)   With regard to living space: mothers of families with above average living space are characterized to a larger extent by:

- less psychological closeness and less understanding of their child.

(iii)   With regard to 'outward signs of social success': more mothers of the families where these signs are most evident are characterized by:

- greater emphasis on training,

- greater concern for the child's socialized and conventional behaviour,

- little concern for the child's spontaneous behaviour.

(iv)   More mothers taking a great interest in classical culture are characterized by:

- little emphasis on training.

(v)   More mothers taking a great interest in <u>popular culture</u> are characterized by:

- more attention paid to the child,

- a fairly objective view of the child,

- average importance given to training

(vi) More mothers taking a great interest in <u>consumer culture</u> are characterized by:

- limited but accurate observation of the child's behaviour,

- reduced psychological proximity to the child, but sound understanding of its behaviour

- special attention given to caring for the child

In short, a comparison between socio-economic and socio-cultural factors on the one hand and attitude variables on the other shows that low and high levels of the former each correspond to a specific pattern of the latter.   Thus there is a <u>connection between socio-economic level and mothers' attitudes</u>, and, to a lesser extent, <u>between socio-cultural level and mothers' attitudes</u>.   But in fact, the three socio-economic factors and the three socio-cultural factors in each case combine in a characteristic way.   It can thus be expected that the pattern of attitude variables linked with these factors will in their turn combine and thereby reinforce or neutralize each other or interact in different ways.

3. Mothers' Attitudes and Children's Development

All specialists in the field of development accept what commonsense has never denied: a child's experiences in the course of its development contribute to shape and to determine this development.   Foremost amongst the factors and components of experience, the <u>behaviour and attitudes of the parents</u> probably play a dominant part, often seen in retrospective clinical studies.

In the 90 families considered in this research, the existence of connections between the mothers' attitudes and the children's level of development is shown by the presence of statistically significant links between the two sets of variables.   Because of the large number of possible combinations, it seemed justified as a first approach to focus on important links between extreme manifestations of mother-attitude variables and extreme scores obtained in the development tests.   Indeed it is not so much the existence of any particular attitude that matters - they are probably all present to some degree - but rather it is the frequency or rarity of these attitudes which is likely to underline connections with the development indices.

From this viewpoint we will consider here only positive or negative linear relations in which the level of developmental variables and the rates of incidence of attitude variables regularly correlate positively or negatively with each other.   There are other, less obvious, links, but they will not be considered here.

3.1 Mothers' attitudes and developmental quotients

Sixteen clear links are recorded between the 5 developmental quotients and the 11 variables related to the mothers' attitudes, as shown in the following table.

TABLE 2 Frequency Levels of the Mothers' Attitude Variables
and Developmental Scores

Level of the mothers' attitude variables		Level of the developmental quotients				
		General	Postural	Coord-ination	Language	Social
Propensity to attribute behavioural characteristics to the child (psychological traits)	S	i	–	–	i	i
	A	–	–	–	–	–
	I	s	–	–	s	s
Expression of restrictive training (demands-prohib-itions-threats etc.)	S	s	s	–	–	–
	A	–	–	–	–	–
	I	i	i	–	–	–
Manifestations of psycho-logical proximity, perception of child's behaviour	S	i	–	–	i	–
	A	–	–	–	–	–
	I	s	–	–	s	–
Manifestation of attention to the child's spontaneous and autonomous behaviour	S	–	–	–	i	i
	A	–	–	–	–	–
	I	–	–	–	s	s
Total of simple,general observations on the child's behaviour	S	–	–	–	–	–
	A	–	–	s	–	–
	I	–	–	i	–	–
Ratio of simple or complex observations	S	–	–	–	s	–
	A	–	–	–	–	–
	I	–	–	–	i	–
Total of incorrect interpretations of child's behaviour	S	–	s	–	–	–
	A	–	–	–	–	–
	I	–	i	–	–	–
Inadequacy of the charact-eristics attributed to the child, and of the inter-pretations of its behaviour	S	–	s	–	–	–
	A	–	–	–	–	–
	I	–	i	–	–	–
Verbal and physical contacts with the child with no other purpose (contact for its own sake)	S	–	–	–	–	–
	A	s	–	–	–	–
	I	i	–	–	–	–
Manifestations of feelings towards the child	S	–	–	–	–	–
	A	–	–	s	–	–
	I	–	–	i	–	–
Explicit or implicit signs of anxiety	S	i	–	–	–	–
	A	–	–	–	–	–
	I	s	–	–	–	–

S = Superior   A = Average   I = Inferior

Broadly speaking, and noting that the different developmental quotients are not necessarily connected with the mothers' attitudes, the table shows that, all things being equal, superior development of the child is often associated with maternal attitudes characterized by:

- a high level of - restrictive training;
                   - simple rather than complex observations;
                   - incorrect interpretations of child behaviour;
                   - attribution of inadequate psychological characteristics
                     to the child, and of inadequate interpretations.

- a low level of   - attribution of behavioural characteristics to the child;
                   - psychological closeness to the child and perception of
                     its behaviour;
                   - attention given to the child's spontaneous and autonomous
                     behaviour;
                   - signs of anxiety.

- an average level of - general simple observations;
                      - contacts for their own sake;
                      - manifestations of feelings.

Inferior development of the child of course corresponds to an inversion of the frequency levels of these mothers' attitudes, those in the last group above appearing at an inferior level.   Less frequent or more ambiguous connections do not seem to contradict these conclusions.

An important result emerges from these findings, about the relation between the child's development and the mothers' attitudes: superior development in young children is frequently associated with a pattern of mothers' attitudes including such features as: a rather poor psychological closeness to the child, little understanding of it, rather superficial and hardly very shrewd observations of its behaviour, mainly spontaneous.   Although these mothers are not loath to have gratuitous contact with the child or to manifest feelings, they seem however to view education as an extremely restrictive and demanding matter.   They are not very anxious.   This general pattern is exactly reversed in the case of inferior development.

As we are here again dealing with a one-to-one relation between variables, it seemed interesting to look at the distribution of the variables of maternal attitudes in the case of the 15 children exhibiting superior development and the 17 children exhibiting inferior development, just as we did for socio-economic and socio-cultural levels.

Looking at the five variables of mothers' attitudes[*] most closely related to the various development quotients, we note the following features: among the 15 children exhibiting superior development, the attitude variables considered appear 31 times at the adequate level, i.e. at the level which corresponds to a superior developmental quotient in the preceding table, and 7 times at the inadequate level, i.e. at the level which corresponds to an inferior developmental quotient.   This phenomenon is less evident in the case of the 17 children exhibiting inferior development;   the attitude variables considered occur 20 times at an adequate level and 12 times at an inadequate level.

---

*The five variables considered here are the first four and the last variable in Table 2.

The one to one relations observed for the entire sample are thus confirmed, particularly in the case of subjects with superior development. The same is true if we examine the number of attitude variables present for the subjects exhibiting superior and inferior development.

TABLE 3   Number of Attitude Variables according to the
Children's Developmental Status

Number of attitude variables present	Among the children	
	Exhibiting superior development (15 children)	Exhibiting inferior development (17 children)
Linked with <u>superior</u> development		
0	2	11
1 or 2	6	4
3 to 5	7	2
Linked with <u>inferior</u> development		
0	9	6
1 or 2	6	9
3 to 5	0	2

Thus, the link between the mothers' attitudes and development status of their children appears very clearly in the extreme cases; however, it seems more marked in the case of more advanced subjects and in the case of attitudes linked with superior development.

3.2   Mothers' attitudes and indices of genetic development

It will be remembered that the method made it possible to rank the subjects according to advance or retardation, with respect to 9 particular aspects of development. Fifteen significant links were found between 9 of the attitude variables and 6 of the developmental variables; advance or retardation in the latter respectively corresponding to the presence of these attitudes on either a superior or an inferior level. The links noted can be summed up as follows in Table 4.

It is surprising to note that it is the ability to discriminate shapes which seems to be most frequently related to attitudes of the mothers. Next come verbal expression and motor coordination of the upper limbs.

Again broadly speaking, this table shows that, all things being equal, advance in the child's genetic development often corresponds to a pattern of mothers' attitudes characterized by:

- a high level of simple rather than complex observation;
- a low level of - psychological closeness and perception of the child's behaviour;
  - interpretations of the child's behaviour;
  - attribution of behavioural characteristics to the child;
  - correct interpretation of the child's behaviour;
  - specific complex observations;
  - signs of anxiety;

- an average or low level of - simple, general observations
                              - 'false' communication.

TABLE 4 Frequency Levels of the Mothers' Attitude Variables and Developmental Advance or Retardation

Level of the mothers' attitude variables		Advance or retardation of the indices of genetic development					
		Discrimination of shapes	Motor Coordination	Verbal Expression	Verbal Comprehension	Association of objects	Reaction
Manifestations of psychological proximity and perception of child behaviour	S	R	R	R	-	-	-
	A	-	-	R	-	-	-
	I	A	A	A	-	-	-
Propensity to attribute behavioural characteristics to the child (psychological traits)	S	-	R	R	R	-	-
	A	-	-	-	-	-	-
	I	-	A	A	A	-	-
Total of interpretations of child behaviour	S	R	R	-	-	-	-
	A	-	-	R	-	-	-
	I	A	A	A	-	-	-
Total of correct interpretations of child behaviour	S	R	-	-	-	-	-
	A	-	-	-	-	-	-
	I	A	-	-	-	-	-
Rate of specific complex observations (limited facts implying deduction)	S	R	-	-	-	-	-
	A	-	-	-	-	-	-
	I	A	-	-	-	-	-
Rate of simple general observations (generalities)	S	-	-	-	-	-	R
	A	-	-	-	-	-	A
	I	-	-	-	-	-	A
Ratio of simple to complex observations	S	A	-	-	-	-	-
	A	-	-	-	-	-	-
	I	R	-	-	-	-	-
'False' communication (threats, deceitful explanations, attitudes)	S	-	-	R	-	-	-
	A	-	-	A	-	-	-
	I	-	-	-	-	-	-
Explicit or implicit signs of anxiety	S	-	-	-	-	R	-
	A	-	-	-	-	-	-
	I	-	-	-	-	A	-

S = Superior   R = Retardation
A = Average   A = Advance
I = Inferior

Retardation in the child's genetic development is of course associated with inverse frequency levels of these attitudes; those of the last group above appearing at a superior level. Beyond these one-to-one relations, we may again wonder how things stand for the individuals by comparing the distribution of the first three attitude variables in the above table (which are most frequently linked with extreme levels of development) for most advanced and most retarded children (i.e. respectively the 12/90 children exhibiting at least 4 indices of advance and the 15/90 children exhibiting at least 4 indices of retardation): among the 12 advanced children the relevant attitude variables appear 17 times at an adequate level, which corresponds to genetic advance in the previous table, and only once on an inadequate level, which corresponds to genetic retardation. We observe similar patterns in the case of the retarded children: the attitude variables appear 14 times on an adequate level, consistent with genetic retardation, and twice at an inadequate level, i.e. the level corresponding to genetic advance.

As for the number of attitude variables per case, it stands as follows:

TABLE 5   Number of Attitude Variables, according to the
Children's Advance or Retardation

Number of attitude variables present	Among the children	
	Most advanced (12 children)	Most retarded (15 children)
Linked with advance 0 1 to 3	2 10	13 2
Linked with retardation 0 1 to 3	11 1	7 8

Thus the connection between the mothers' attitudes and genetic development in particular areas is confirmed by the extreme groups. However, just as in the case of developmental quotients, the relation seems to be more marked for the advanced subjects and for the mothers' attitudes linked with developmental advance.

3.3   Mothers' attitudes and indices of harmony and coherence

As we said before, the index of harmony of development reflects the degree of homogeneity existing between the 4 specific developmental quotients; the coherence indices reflect for each of the developmental quotients the difference between the age at which all items are passed, and the age corresponding to the highest item passed by the subject.

Although related to the child's development, these new variables reveal a developmental feature quite different from the performance levels measured by the developmental quotients or the indices of genetic developments previously mentioned. These variables indeed refer to the homogeneity of the results achieved by the same child in the baby-tests. A given level of harmony or coherence can be found with superior, average or inferior development. A high level of harmony or coherence indicates minimal dispersion of results for a particular area of development. A low level indicates a high degree of dispersion and reflects the fact that the level achieved is the result of a scattering of performances over the scale. It can thus be expected that developmental levels and degrees of homogeneity are relatively independent of each other; and this is confirmed by looking at the distribution of the indices of harmony and coherence for the 15 subjects exhibiting superior development and for the 17 subjects exhibiting inferior development, as previously defined.

What about the links between homogeneity of development and mothers' attitudes? We note 19 significant relations between the 5 indices of homogeneity and 12 attitude variables as shown in table 6.

It is interesting to see that the coherence index for the quotient of social development does not seem to be related to the mothers' attitude variables. Ignoring this, and from a global point of view which neglects the details of the relations between indices, it appears from the table that the homogeneity of the child's development often corresponds to a pattern of mothers' attitudes characterized by:

- an average or high level of
    correct interpretation of child behaviour;
    particular complex observations;
    interpretations of child behaviour;
    contact with the child for its own sake;
    stimulating training in the total of training manifestations;
    implicit or explicit signs of anxiety

- a low level of
    simple observations in comparison with complex observations;
    manifestations of stimulating training;
    manifestations of restrictive training;
    general complex observations;
    concern for the child conforming and having a conventional behaviour;
    inadequacy of the characteristics attributed to the child and of the
    interpretations of its behaviour

Heterogeneity of the developmental indices is associated with an inversion of the frequency levels of these attitudes, the first appearing at an inferior level and the second at a superior level.

Thus a high degree of developmental homogeneity is associated with such features as the accurate and precise observation of the child's behaviour, correct interpretation of it, which implies good psychological proximity and great attention towards the child, as is proved by the presence of contacts for their own sake. On the other hand, insistence on the training aspects is minimal essentially, not restrictive but clearly stimulating, as the concern for the child's conformity is limited.   Lastly, a high rate of anxiety is apparent.   The opposite pattern is associated with a high degree of heterogeneity in the child's development. These relations lead to an important and perhaps rather unexpected conclusion: the patterns of mothers' attitudes that go with homogeneity and heterogeneity of the developmental indices are almost the exact opposite of the patterns that go respectively with superior or inferior development.   Indeed, either the attitude variables linked with the indices of development levels are not the same as those linked with the homogeneity indices, and vice versa (and they have the opposite psychological value) or when they are the same, the relationships to the development levels and the harmony or coherence indices have the opposite sign, except in the case of 'contact for its own sake' where the direction is the same for the developmental levels and for homogeneity.

TABLE 6 Frequency Level of the Mothers' Attitude Variables and Homogeneity of the Child's Performances

Level of the Mothers' Attitude Variables		Harmony	Coherence of the various developmental indices				
			General	Postural	Coordination	Verbal	Social
Total of correct interpretations of child behaviour	S	-	-	-	s	-	-
	A	s	s	-	-	-	-
	I	i	i	-	i	-	-
Rate of specific complex observations (limited facts implying deduction)	S	s	s	-	-	-	-
	A	s	-	-	-	-	-
	I	i	i	-	-	-	-
Ratio of simple to complex observations	S	i	i	-	-	-	-
	A	-	-	-	-	-	-
	I	s	s	-	-	-	-
Total of interpretations of child behaviour	S	-	-	-	-	-	-
	A	-	-	s	-	s	-
	I	-	-	i	-	i	-
Expressions of stimulating training (encouragement, stimulation, demonstrations)	S	-	-	i	-	i	-
	A	-	-	-	-	-	-
	I	-	-	s	-	s	-
Verbal and physical contact with the child, with no other purpose (contact for its own sake)	S	s	-	-	-	s	-
	A	-	-	-	-	i	-
	I	i	-	-	-	i	-
Ratio of stimulating on total signs of training	S	-	-	-	-	-	-
	A	-	s	-	-	-	-
	I	-	i	-	-	-	-
Signs of restrictive training (demands, prohibitions, threats etc)	S	-	-	-	-	i	-
	A	-	-	-	-	-	-
	I	-	-	-	-	s	-
Rate of general, complex observations (generalities implying deduction)	S	-	i	-	-	-	-
	A	-	-	-	-	-	-
	I	-	s	-	-	-	-
Manifestation of attention given to conformity, obedience, politeness, discipline &c	S	-	-	-	-	i	-
	A	-	-	-	-	-	-
	I	-	-	-	-	s	-
Inadequacy of the characteristics attributed to the child, and of the interpretation of its behaviour	S	-	-	-	-	i	-
	A	-	-	-	-	-	-
	I	-	-	-	-	s	-
Explicit or implicit signs of anxiety	S	-	s	-	-	-	-
	A	-	-	-	-	-	-
	I	-	i	-	-	-	-

i = inferior
s = superior

3.4 Conclusions

(i)   The main conclusion to be drawn from this section is undoubtedly that mothers' attitudes have more bearing on the child's developmental status, and on the harmony and coherence of this development than do the socio-economic or socio-cultural factors peculiar to the family environment.   This hypothesis is indeed consistent with common sense and clinical experience as well as with genetic psychology.

(ii)   The variables of mothers' attitudes which happen to be related to the developmental level or to homogeneity are mainly: the degree of psychological closeness between mother and child, the mother's attention and sensibility to the child's behaviour, the quantity, nature and orientation of supposed 'educational' manifestations, the rate of contact for its own sake, the signs of anxiety and the manifestation of feelings.

(iii) At first sight, the connections do not reveal any contradictions as far as the relationships among these groups of indices are concerned, which contributes to give real consistency to the observed links.

(iv)   An analysis of the links prompts us to assume that for the age groups considered, there are two basic patterns of maternal attitudes:

- the first would be characterized by a lower degree of attention to and understanding of the child, a smaller degree of psychological closeness to the child;
   mothers would concentrate on education, conformity and performance; this
   pattern often goes with a superior developmental level; the reverse pattern
   being associated with an inferior developmental level.

- the second pattern would characterize more attentive, understanding, and
   receptive mothers, who are psychologically closer to their children, who are
   also more anxious, and show greater concern and respect for their nature,
   their possibilities and their limitations.   This pattern is associated with
   more harmony and coherence in the development; the reverse pattern going
   with heterogeneous development.

The fact that these two patterns contradict and exclude one another seems to indicate that the pattern of attitudes associated with superior development does not fit in with a homogeneous development of the child and that the pattern associated with inferior development does not fit in with a heterogeneous development.

4.   The Questionnaire

The above relationships represent a global approach to the facts.   In view of the nature and the interest of the results obtained for the whole sample, it seems useful to distinguish the different genetic stages (10 months, 15 months, and 21 months) included in the sample.   The global connections are likely to conceal other connections which are specific to a given age.   Some attitude variables are, as a matter of fact, significantly a function of age.   It is possible that some parental attitudes, which vary according to socio-economic and cultural factors, emerge earlier in some groups than in others, at a more or a less favourable stage in the child's development.   It is also possible that, in function of these same variational factors, some of the parental attitudes themselves brought about some ways of behaving, whereas in other cases, these same attitudes would appear later as a response to the child's development.

To illustrate this approach, which takes the genetic stages into account, results will be given pertaining to some variables from the questionnaire.   One general observation, however, is in order - compared with the connections considered previously, the variables of mothers' attitude derived from the questionnaire, when confronted with the test results, reveal a surprisingly small number of significant relationships; in addition it seems here that the socio-cultural factors play a more important part than do the socio-economic factors. On the other hand, the number of developmental variables which have significant links with the socio-economic and socio-cultural factors seems larger in the case of variables from the questionnaire than in the case of variables from the test results.

This can perhaps be partly explained by the fact that the variables considered now are indices related to socio-affective development and are in no way connected with general development. These remarks also prompt us to believe that the absence of differences recorded in most investigations into the influence of the socio-economic environment on the child's development before the age of two years is perhaps due to the nature of the instruments used and the kind of information collected.

4.1 Relationships between parental attitudes and socio-economic or cultural factors

The following variables are taken into consideration:
- the frequency of parent's assistance to the child;
- the fact that the parent helps the child when asked;
- the fact that the parent lets the child manage by itself.

For the 90 families, frequency of parents' assistance to the child is not significantly linked with the child's age, but it related to the factors 'outward signs of social success'(p=.01) and 'popular culture' (p=.02). The families exhibiting little 'outward signs of social success' are characterized by a high percentage of answers ranked in the extreme classes, which is perhaps a sign of the heterogeneity of their educational behaviour.

In the same way, regardless of the child's age, parents in the medium or top group for 'popular culture' often let the child manage by itself (p=.10).

Things are somewhat different when we consider the parents' reactions to an appeal for help on the part of the child. It is obvious that the number of positive responses from the parents grows with the child's age (p=.001). Moreover, the crossing of this variable with the different socio-economic and socio-cultural factors gives no significant information for the whole sample. Do the results obtained for all the children aged 10, 15 and 21 months remain valid for each of the age-groups?

Table 7 shows that the parents with high socio-economic status respond more frequently and at an earlier stage in a positive way to the demands of the child. It also reveals a progressive improvement of the assistance behaviour in low socio-economic groups, and a similar pattern of development of this behaviour in average and low groups.

The influence of the socio-economic factor is of particular importance when the child is 15 months old. The difference between the two extreme groups (low and high level) is significant at a probability level of .02 (Finey-Latscha).

We can now ask ourselves the meaning of such a finding. If parents with high socio-economic status always respond positively to the demands of a 15-month-old child, is this a result of the way this child formulates its demand (we might imagine, for example, verbal advance on the part of these children) or rather of the way the parent interprets this demand (greater empathy on the part of the parent toward the child)?

TABLE 7   Assistance to the Child, according to its Age and
            Socio-economic Level

Assistance upon request	Age			
	10mths	15mths	21mths	Total
Yes Socio-economic level: low average high	3) 3) 11 5)	5) 8) 23 10)	10) 9) 29 10)	18) 20) 63 25)
No Socio-economic level: low average high	7) 7) 19 5)	5) 2) 7 0)	0) 1) 1 0)	12) 10) 27 5)

In the same way, for parents with low socio-economic status, are the variations the result of the child's less frequent appeals, or of the attitude of the parents who are not prone to pay attention to the child?   Last but not least, do these changes in attitude according to age and socio-economic status affect the child's development?

This shows how important it is, in seeking to answer these questions, that we work with groups of children which are as homogeneous as possible with respect to age or sex as well as with respect to developmental levels.   We tried out this multidimensional approach to the question of parents looking at picture-books with their children, a behaviour obviously depending on age, but nevertheless appearing earlier in the high socio-economic group.   A detailed investigation has shown that families of higher socio-economic status apparently introduce picture-books at a relatively early stage (10 or 15 months), but they do not take the child's developmental level into consideration.   The families of a lower socio-economic status only introduce picture-books later on (15 or 21 months) and this particularly when the child shows a satisfactory level of development.

Thus, we could say that circumstances vary according to the socio-economic level. Parents of a low socio-economic status do not begin to look at picture-books with the child before it has achieved a certain level of verbal development: so, in a way, it is the child who, because of his development, induces the educational practice.   Parents of a high socio-economic status, on the contrary, introduce this practice at an earlier stage, regardless of the child's verbal level; in a way, the socio-economic level is the trigger for the appearance of the educational behaviour.

These results prompt us to believe that the processes involved in either case are qualitatively different.   An examination of the mother's activity as she shows the picture-book to the child, confirms this hypothesis: parents of a high socio-economic status much more frequently ask the child to look at the book or to listen to the story, whereas parents of a low socio-economic status rather ask the child to repeat the name of the picture or to give a name to the picture.

4.2 Relationships between variables pertaining to the child's behaviour and socio-economic or cultural factors

Besides the study of the variables pertaining to the parents' attitudes, the questionnaire also takes into consideration some of the child's ways of behaving, which cannot be evaluated within the context of the testing.   Only those variables related to emotional behaviour such as Laughing or Crying are mentioned in this report.   These variables, codified according to the different genetic stages, are defined, on the one hand, by the variety of the situations which, according to the parents, prompt the child to laugh or cry, and, on the other hand, by the parents' explicit answer to a question on what they feel to be the frequency of tears and laughter.

Broadly speaking, if we consider the sample as a whole, families of low socio-economic status are characterized by a greater variety of situations prompting the child to cry than families of high socio-economic status.   Mothers from deprived environments feel that their children cry frequently.   Emotional behaviour like laughing did not appear to depend on socio-economic factors, whereas the links with cultural factors are often significant.   In this respect, laughter constitutes a behavioural response often occurring in the families showing a high level of 'classical culture', or a low level of 'popular culture'.

A comparison of the different data concerning the child's laughter or crying suggests that a low level of emotional reaction prevails in children from families characterized by a low level of popular culture.   However, in view of the method used to collect this information, these features could be explained by the parents' lack of sensitivity to the child's emotional life.   In other words, the ambiguity of the results could either indicate the poorness or instability of the emotional behaviour of children from families characterized by a low level of popular culture, or equally, it could indicate the parents' limited involvement in the child's life.

To conclude, all these observations prompt us to believe that educational practices appear at different ages and in different ways, according to the socio-economic status of the family.   The examples we have just given stress the need to go beyond the global relationships which appear in a first analysis.   Work thus remains to be done, which will undoubtedly bring to light some up to now hidden influences.

3 The Investigation - Action in the Crèche

1. Purpose and Motivation of the Experiment

In connection with the research we have just described, a psychologist experienced in the field of early childhood has been able to participate during two and a half years, in the life of the crèche of Anderlecht, the same commune from which the sample of 90 families was taken. The head of this establishment, interested in research and innovation, had asked for this collaboration. This is not so much a research project in the academic sense of the word, as an attempt to involve a research oriented psychologist in an innovating scheme undertaken in the framework of a given institution.

The basic idea behind this action corresponds to the general objective of the research: if the origins of socio-cultural handicap are to be found in early childhood, they should perhaps be sought not only in the family but in the crèche, which is mainly attended by children from less privileged environments. Psychological observation of this particular environment might lay bare possible influences handicapping the child's further development; psychological action in this environment might change it so that it favours the child's development.

Not only is the number of crèches in this country much too small, but, in general, they show little concern for the mental health and developmental harmony of young children. The children live there, in a closed community, a microcosm secluded from the outside world. The crèche is rarely in contact with families and never with those institutions which will take care of the children in the future: the pre-kindergartens and the nursery schools. There is discontinuity among the child's initial educational environments.

The training of the staff is inadequate and the child nursing studies are neither highly thought of nor fully professional. Moreover, students choose to train at about the age of fifteen, and the diploma is awarded three years later. We may ask whether such students are mature enough and whether their motivations are clear enough at this stage of their adolescence. This perhaps explains why the nursery nurses see themselves more as nursery aids than as educators of early childhood, responsible for the integration of their educational attitudes with the perspective of each child's family. Hardly aware of their responsibility towards the child, they are very often ignorant of the critical and sometimes irreversible influence they may have on a child's future development. They take little part in the child's emotional life, and impose ways of behaving in their own interest, rather than adapting their own behaviour to the individuality of each child.   In a word, their conception of early childhood is very traditional, and their concern for education usually barely apparent and often completely absent.

2. The Psychologist's Action

The general orientation the psychologist wanted to give to his action in the crèche can be summarised as follows:

(i)   to organise a systematic detection, compensation and prevention of possible retardation or deviations in psychological and psychomotor development of the children;

(ii)   to induce the crèche to adapt itself to the individual nature of each child: individuality of psychological development, and individuality of the family environment;

(iii)   to make each child benefit from the enriching experience, which community life can bring, and to foster his socialization;

(iv)   to enhance the staff's perception of the value of their role, by making them autonomous and responsible, this essentially being to make up for their lack of motivation and their poor knowledge of children, which impedes real individualized relationships;

(v)   to ensure that family and crèche work together by starting a dialogue, promoting mutual knowledge, an exchange on all levels, and by involving the families in the life of the crèche through direct participation, and of the crèche in family life through mutual respect;

(vi)   to devise new ways of educating young children in groups.

In short, the general aim of the psychologist's action can be summed up in the phrase 'Individualization - Familiarization - Socialization'.   His participation in the life of the crèche aimed to bring about, in the long run, changes, and induce the crèche itself to modify its structure and the way it works.

In more concrete terms, the psychologist's enterprise can be summed up under five headings, for each of which some illustrative examples are given in what follows.

2.1 Influencing the nursery nurses[*]

Originally, nursery nurses had a set routine of daily tasks to perform, and limited themselves to these.   They took little interest in the child as an individual, did not know the children in their room very well (which was due to frequent changes) and had poor contacts with the families, even when such contacts were possible - they were afraid of meeting some of the mothers, and took an authoritarian attitude towards others.   They rarely took initiatives.

---

[*]In the following text, we used the term 'nursery nurse' for the staff taking care of the children's welfare.

There was little communication among the nursery nurses, and none at all between them and the management. The nurses frequently complained about their working conditions, but never tried to change them. They reproached the management for not visiting the rooms, for not informing them about plans, not consulting them, frequently changing their assignments and not taking any interest in them. But these reproaches were never clearly formulated to the management.

The psychologist tried to encourage the nurses to express themselves by being daily and individually in contact with them in the rooms, by taking part in their duties, and by eating with them in the dining room.

Moreover, he introduced termly 'case conferences' with the nurses about each child's development, to make them aware of the methods of observation and of the concept of development. These meetings gradually helped the nurses systematically to adapt the activities they undertook to the children's real needs. The idea was not to establish a 'curriculum', but rather, as spontaneously as possible to provide each child with appropriate stimulation at the right time. Thus the aim was not to practise a form of early childhood pedagogy, but to foster attitudes centred on individual development and which would complement and extend the education given by the family without taking its place.

2.2 Influencing the staff

The psychologist tried to foster a dialogue between management and staff by facilitating the organisation of weekly meetings and of full (but voluntary) monthly staff meetings, dealing with practical and professional questions as well as with psychological and educational problems concerning the children.

The psychologist also took part in staff meetings of a more technical nature, where he tried to answer the explicit questions in a less neutral and more critical way than in the case of the nursery nurses, without however confining himself to a well defined technical role.

2.3 Influencing the families

Without seeking regular contact with the families, on account of the short-term nature of the experiment, the psychologist nevertheless systematically discussed with the staff the problem of the family, within the framework that pre-school education was a complement to and not a substitute for the family. He tried to make each person aware of his own responsibility in this matter and of the necessity of collaboration. A proposal by the management, with the approval of the staff, concentrated the crèche action in 1973 on the theme 'the family in the crèche'. Parents were allowed to come into the rooms on certain occasions, among others on Mother's Day and at Christmas, when the nursery nurses organised small receptions in each room.

With the same idea in mind, the annual toy exhibitions which had been organised for many years for the parents were now opened to the public generally, so as to inform them. The press and television paid considerable attention to this.

2.4 Influencing the children

The psychologist took an active part in the prevention, detection and compensation of behavioural retardations or deviations (from the viewpoint of normal healthy development rather than from the frequent 'pathological' approach).

- prevention
  by making the nurses aware of the concept of development, of methods of

observation and certain techniques of activity.   This last point in particular
was the result of friendly rivalry which developed between the rooms, once a
certain team spirit had appeared.   Gradually, the nurses responsible for a
room took turns to present to their colleagues new activities which they had
conceived and worked out with their group.   An 'activities' bank' was thus
created.

- detection
  thanks to increasingly keen observation by the nurses, who became more and
  more aware of certain aspects of behaviour and of their meaning, through
  direct observation of their children;   thanks to staff meetings, and,
  gradually, thanks to the better contacts between the nurses and the parents.
  The collaboration of the physiotherapist proved particularly valuable in this
  regard.

- compensation
  by making the staff aware of the individual features of each child's development, which call for an individualized attitude on their part;
  by playing down certain situations (mutism, anorexia, aggressiveness,
  difficulties in sphincter control...) which very frequently left the nurses
  completely at a loss.   By his reassurance and explanations of certain situations, the psychologist helped the staff to deal with these problems in more
  rational ways, and to find more practical solutions, as much for the sake of
  the children's adjustment as for their own;
  by taking part in certain individual treatments, in collaboration with the
  doctor, and, frequently, with the physiotherapist;
  and eventually, by bringing the families to take part in individual treatment.
  This also began by reassurance and playing down.

Progress was often noted in the children's behaviour after a few weeks of treatment.   This progress was evaluated and made objective for the nurses with the
help of the Brunet-Lézine developmental scale.

The efforts of the psychologist also aimed at introducing some masculine presence
in the crèche, which is essential, and at making the nurses more attentive to
body language and expressive gesture, which are generally disregarded but which
are very important in the communication between infants and their educators.

2.5 Influencing the institution

The psychologist helped with the decentralization project set in motion by the
Head of the 'Centre Communal de la Petite Enfance' in Anderlecht.   This took the
form of 'mini-crèches' geographically better spread.   He contributed in particular to the architectural design of the buildings and of their equipment, to
building up the team spirit of the staff, and to the creation of 'vertical'
groupings of mixed ages, which offer undeniable practical and educational
advantages.

3. Results of the Action

It is not possible to provide numerical evidence on the effectiveness of the
psychologist's work in the crèche, but it is nonetheless interesting to list some
of the favourable changes which came about in the institution during the time he
was present.   Although he does not claim at all to be the originator of these
changes, there are however reasons to believe that he largely contributed to
bring them about.   We note among others the following changes:

- Monthly meetings of the whole staff;   presence of the nurses concerned at the
  staff meetings;   direct participation of all the staff in decision-making..

- Participation of the nurse responsible for a room (a newly created function) in the weekly meetings.

- Acceptance by the management that staff meetings should be held during working hours (groups of a dozen nurses).

- The nurses in each room make their weekly timetable as a team.   The timetable is no longer imposed from above.   In the past this has often aroused dissatisfaction and even jealousy amongst the nurses.

- The suppression of uniform working clothes for the personnel.

- The nurses became aware of the shortcomings of their professional training. (This resulted in trade union action on the part of the Anderlecht nurses to obtain a better training;   the union, at first surprised and rather at a loss at being confronted with a claim which had nothing to do with working hours or salary, pushed this problem up to national level.)

- The participation of a group of nurses (about 20) in a conference organized by the World Organization for Preschool Education at Mons, on the theme 'The Training of the Nursery Nurse'.   On the initiative of the nurses, a preparatory work group was formed in Anderlecht.   Four nurses reported on its work at the conference.

- The nurses took part in the organisation of toy exhibitions.   Several of them made toys out of easily available materials to show parents some creative possibilities.   Others conducted a workshop for toy-making.

- The nurses were authorised to decide themselves whether or not the child needs a bath on its arrival.   This bath on arrival is thus no longer compulsory for all.   This makes it possible to slow down the rhythm of bathing, and consequently to improve the contact with children in this intimate relationship. In addition, nurses are allowed to give the bath in the course of the day, when a child needs one or when the nurse has the time.

- It is no longer compulsory to take children's temperature on arrival in the morning.   The thermometer is now only used when the nurse suspects the child has a temperature.

- Curtains on inside windows of the rooms have been taken down at the nurses' request, and they now work in full view.   The children too can take a somewhat greater part in the life of the building.

- Organization of a weekly meeting to introduce new arrivals.   Each week, new children enter the crèche.   Social workers make a preliminary investigation and visit the child's home at least once.   The information collected is the basis of a child's file, which is only used when the child shows difficulties during its time in the crèche.   Thus the information is not systematically used.   Since May 1973, at the request of the nurses, most of the information is communicated to them orally by the social service, during a meeting. Both the child and the family are described.   Consequently nurses are able to greet them in a more satisfactory way when they enter the crèche.

- Organization of a 'transfer card' system for the kindergarten or nursery school when the child leaves the crèche.   The card mentions the child's medical history, the structure of its development as well as information about family background and general behaviour.   These cards are discussed in group but are drawn up by the doctor.

- The parents are allowed into the rooms to play with the children or talk to the nurses before the medical examination.

- The organization of meetings with the parents on Mother's Day and Christmas.

- Files are set up for each child containing typical pieces of work (scribbles, scrap-book, stitchings, drawings...) which will be given to the parents when the child leaves the crèche.   These files stimulate the creativity of the nurses, who actively look for new types of activities, and they reinforce relationships between family and crèche as well as illustrating the child's development.

On the whole, these various modifications suggest a number of conclusions:

(1) A new'structure of collective education, complementary to the family and integrated with it', has appeared: the open mini-crèche;

(2) more and more initiatives are taken by the staff;

(3) these initiatives are accepted and encouraged by the management;

(4) the staff works with genuine team spirit;

(5) a real effort has been made to individualize the contact with the child;

(6) the crèche becomes more and more open to a dialogue with the parents;

(7) the staff is aware of how much more there is to be learned, and wants to benefit from continuous training;

(8) the spirit of the work and the philosophy of the crèche are as much concerned with an educative role as they are with medico-social care. The crèche has begun to realise that it has more to offer to the child than mere physical security.   The nurses want to become 'preschool educators'.

4. Conclusions

The action which has been carried out shows, at least through the development of the 'Centre Communal de la Petite Enfance' that the 'crèche' institution in Belgium can be largely improved!

- with regard to its <u>structure</u>: decentralisation, reduction in size, vertical grouping, open crèche...

- with regard to the <u>staff</u>: team spirit, reform of the training of nursery nurses, in-service training, introduction of psychologists...

- with regard to the <u>spirit</u> of the crèche: cooperation with the families, a centre of dissemination, of training, of information and of preventive work...

The project also shows the effectiveness in the creche of a psychologist spec- ialized in early childhood, and integrated with the team of adults.   This need not necessarily be a full-time job, except perhaps in the beginning.   Later on, the psychologist could work a few hours per week in the crèche - direct contact with the nurses in their rooms, individual examinations of the children, participation in meetings, accessibility to the staff, the families and the management, etc.

Conclusion

A. Within the limits imposed by the instruments used and by the way we used them, it appears that at the age of 10, 15 and 21 months, the differences between children from privileged and the children from deprived socio-economic environments, with regard to psychological development are not obvious, and in some respects, are unexpected. At these ages, the behaviour of children from deprived socio-economic environments does not reveal any sign of a psychological handicap or of the possibility of a later appearance of such a handicap. On the contrary, these children usually show a slight advance as far as locomotion is concerned.

The importance of the factor 'living space' evidenced by the present research, should be stressed. It appears indeed that an average living space often goes with a good quotient of general development, and that inferior space is often associated with good development of coordination.

B. The variables of mothers' attitudes, as defined by a content analysis of the mothers' interviews, are much more sensitive to the socio-economic and socio-cultural factors considered than are the developmental variables. Here, the socio-economic factors appear to be much more important than socio-cultural factors.

Socio-economic differences and, to a lesser extent, socio-cultural differences undeniably affect the attitudes of the mothers, and consequently the type and quality of the child's experiences. Economic and cultural factors of course combine in a different way in each family.

We have described two major patterns of mothers' attitudes which are connected both with economic and cultural factors, and with developmental variables; consequently it seems justifiable to consider the mothers' attitudes as intermediate variables between economic and cultural factors on the one hand, and developmental variables on the other.

C. The absence of important differences between children according to their environments, which was mentioned under A, seems to indicate that the variables of mothers' attitudes related to economic and cultural factors have no perceptible impact at the ages considered. This, however, does not rule out the possibility of later medium or long term consequences.

This was what Geneviève Roger(1) attempted to investigate in a follow-up study of 30 children taken from the original sample. It seems appropriate to include some of her main findings in the present conclusions.

Ten children from each socio-economic level (inferior, average, superior) were studied about one and a half years later when the average age of the children was 2.9 years. There were two important findings:

(1) for the Terman-Merrill test, the average IQ of the 10 children from an inferior socio-economic environment was 117, that of the 10 children from a superior socio-economic environment was 136; this difference being significant (p=.05).

(2) The comparison of the ranking of the children according to Brunet-Lézine score, and the ranking according to the Terman-Merrill test, six months later, shows that amongst the ten children from an inferior socio-economic environment, this rank has improved in 3 cases and has worsened in 7 cases, whereas in the case of the children from a superior socio-economic environment the figures are respectively 9 and 1, the difference between these two groups being significant (p=.02).

It is thus obvious that children from an inferior socio-economic environment are differentiating unfavourably from those from a superior socio-economic environment - the 'socio-cultural handicap' is beginning to take shape.

This conclusion is largely confirmed by using 'developmental indices' similar to those used in the research, but which are now defined in the context of the Terman test. Here, too, important differences emerge, to the detriment of children from inferior socio-economic environments, particularly with respect to coordination of the upper limbs, recognition of graphic symbols, and verbal expression. In the original research, there was no such differentiation between the two groups on these variables.

G. Roger's study shows that, if certain children just begin preschool at the moment of the investigation, this factor, which is independent of the family's socio-economic status, cannot possibly account for the gap which is widening.

When she takes into consideration the children from both inferior and superior environments having an IQ above or below the average of their respective groups, G. Roger finds appreciable differences with respect to the mothers' attitudes noted one and a half years before. Regardless of the socio-economic level, mothers whose children have high IQ's are mainly those who have warm, hardly punitive attitudes, and a tendency to foster the child's experiences. On the contrary, the mothers of the children who have low IQ's can mainly be characterized by strict educational attitudes, a lack of warmth, and a tendency to limit the child's experiences.

Although these findings concern only 16 children from the original sample, (9 children from an inferior environment, 7 from a superior environment), they nevertheless are of the utmost importance. They reveal the existence of a link between the mothers' attitudes predominant between the ages of 10 and 21 months and the level of psychological development reached by the children one and a half years later. In addition, these contrasting mothers' attitudes are very much like the two attitude patterns we were able to identify in the original research. Curiously, however, their bearing on development has been reversed. The attitude thought to go with favourable development between the ages of 10 and 21 months, turns out to go with inferior development between the ages of 2 and 3 years, and vice versa.

In short, it is not unlikely that we may have isolated at least one of the factors probably explaining the way socio-cultural handicap works - the patterns of mothers' attitudes predominant in the initial development of the child.

D. The action undertaken in the creche has proved fruitful. It is possible to improve the quality of this institution by taking judicious measures, and to increase its educational value. It is possible, through a psycho-pedagogic approach, to raise the level of the nurses' qualifications and involvement, to modify their attitudes and, in particular, to develop attitudes of the 'proximity-contact' type, and to moderate behaviour of the 'training-priority' type.

It must be possible a fortiori, and even prior to school education, to modify mothers' attitudes by similar means, mainly aimed at reducing attitudes likely to favour socio-cultural handicaps. In this respect, we should think of:

- preparing young couples for parenthood;

- making widely available information for young parents and future parents;

- organizing contact and discussion groups for parents, on a local basis or on the basis of affinity;

- training teams of 'family visitors' qualified in the field of family education (similar to health visitors in the field of health).

This kind of work could start from pre-peri- and post-natal clinics, from creches, or from the early childhood centres or similar institutions, on condition that those involved should have specific training that would give them real psychological, educational and family qualifications.

REFERENCE

(1) Roger, Geneviève. 'Influence du niveau socio-économique familial sur le développement du jeune enfant'   Memoire de licence, U.L.B., 1975.

Part 2
From Compensation to Educational Innovation

Summary of the research undertaken by the Laboratorium voor
Ontwikkelingspsychologie, Rijksuniversiteit Gent, in close
collaboration with the Centre for Developmental Psychology
(subsidised, at the initiative of the Minister, by the Collective
Fundamental Research Fund) and the Educational Centre of the
City of Ghent.

Prof. W. De Coster
Dr. A. de Meyer

Researchers: R. Doom, L. Heyerick,
I. Mervielde, G. Redant,
P. Van Geert, A. Vynckier

Social workers: M. Lievens, L. Van Eeckel

Pre-school teachers: R. De Coninck, C. Gillade,
J. Van Cauwenberghe,
M. Vermassen, M. Vermeir

Introduction

If we examine educational statistics, we will be struck by how few working-class children gain entry to higher education and forms of education preparatory to this. Moreover, the high failure rate amongst these children at primary school level, where it begins, is striking.

These problems became a source of great interest in the 60's. Many compensatory or remedial strategies were elaborated and applied with varying degrees of success. This once more raised the century old nature/nurture controversy; are the differences in school attainment between social classes due more to heredity than to environment?

Let us first consider what those defending the heredity argument have to say. School results may well be strongly influenced by culture, but this is less so for some IQ tests. Heredity estimates for non-verbal IQ tests are extremely high; and the average IQ is an excellent predictor of school success; consequently, it should come as no surprise that there is a connection between social status and scholastic achievement. Moreover, due to the social mobility so marked in our society, the differences tend to be stable.

The environmentalists question the scientific value of heredity estimates. They maintain that there are too many alternative explanations. In the first place, the life styles of people from different social classes vary greatly. This is matched by a different cultural pattern; the school only embraces the cultural pattern of the 'higher' social levels. It is bad policy anyway - they claim - automatically to regard differences as inferiorities or retardation.

We have purposely presented both standpoints in a very schematic way. A careful study was made of authors supporting each of these viewpoints, but this failed to clarify the issue. Too many questions remained unanswered; the argument frequently lacks subtlety.

It would seem to be of little use to pursue the controversy further. The truth doubtless lies somewhere in between. We can influence the environment; and even those who rate hereditary influences high admit that there is some scope. Estimates of genetic influence on IQ are in any case higher than those for school results.

But there is more. Estimates of the influence of hereditary factors in any case

41

invariably refer to an existing situation. If the environment, the school environment for example, is improved, we can expect almost all children to profit by this. If, in addition, we differentiate more within the classroom, we will undoubtedly be able to set minimal attainable objectives for the whole school population, instead of subjecting slow learners to repeated failure, as at present. Thus, we feel that our Interaction Research has far more to offer than the study of the respective parts played by environment and heredity in the development of various skills.

The Ghent project was carried out with children from the 2nd, and more particularly from the 3rd year of the kindergarten (4- and 5-year olds). Is the chosen age-group in fact the best? We consider that to provide increased stimulus for very young children is an appropriate and fruitful exercise. Intervention in both the home and the crèche frequently proves to be profitable. Our own investigation in fact clearly indicates how great the influence of the crèche can be. But notwithstanding the importance of the first few years of the child's life, much can still be done after the child has entered primary school. At these levels, problems of evaluation are encountered. As will be seen in this report, we attach great importance to evaluation research; very few effective evaluation techniques relevant to young children are available.

The research project described in the following pages grew out of typical compensatory education and aimed to transform this into educational innovation.

In the first phase we took as a starting point the programmes which had been tried elsewhere outside Belgium, and which are concerned with introducing skills which have, or appear to have, immediate relevance to formal schooling. The results proved unreliable. The first experimental group made clear gains, but when the programme was repeated with a second group, the gains were less; nor did they have any lasting effect.

We came to the conclusion that ultimately we were evaluating more than the programme itself. The enthusiasm of the teacher, the physical infrastructure, and the guidance given are a few of the variables which can explain the variability of the success rate.

Accordingly, we made radical changes in our methods of operation. In the first place, the teachers were involved more intensively in the project. We collaborated to improve the broader educational context. A programme to give the teacher the opportunity to make radical changes in classroom management was drawn up.

It was only after this change had been realised that we began to rethink our compensatory strategies. We interpreted 'compensation' as 'specific help for children who failed to achieve objectives laid down by the programme'.

The results are most encouraging. It should be emphasised that this is in no small measure due to the fact that relationships between teachers and researchers have been greatly improved.

1 The Compensation Programme 1970-1973

Between 1970 and 1973 we worked on the development, execution and evaluation of a compensatory programme. Its aim was to minimise retardation in working-class children by intervening at the pre-school level. The programme concentrated principally on the development of perceptual and motor skills and language - the latter mainly because of its presumed relevance to cognitive development. With reference to these two areas, two parts can be distinguished in the programme: a perceptual-motor programme, based on the work of M. Frostig (1) and a cognitive programme based on a number of Dutch programmes (Kohnstamm, Utrecht Compensation Programme, Gerstel, Haarlem activation-programme).

The objectives and content, application and evaluation are each discussed below.

1. Objectives and Content

The objectives of the two programmes cannot always be easily separated. The language exercises are always based on observation, but speech and thought were also stimulated in the perceptual-motor programme.

1.1 The perceptual-motor programme

The programme has five parts:

(a) Eye-motor co-ordination: development of the ability to co-ordinate vision with the movements of the body, or with a part or parts of the body (gross and fine motor co-ordination, and so on).

(b) Figure-ground discrimination: development of the ability to concentrate on one object within the entire field of observation and learning to see the relation between that object and its background (differentiation of objects in a room, in a picture; differentiation of different objects, and so on).

(c) Form constancy: development of the ability to observe that an object has a number of immutable characteristics, irrespective of the changing impressions recorded by the retina (classification of shapes according to size, arranging them according to shape, transformation from two to three dimensional space, and so on).

(d) Perception of position in space: development of body schema; relation of the body to other objects, differentiation between left and right, and so on.

(e) Perception of spatial relations: copying patterns, ability to relate objects to each other in a certain way, etc.

The skills enumerated above were developed by means of games centred on a topic of interest (exercises in three-dimensional space).   This is alternated with worksheets.   Both the game-exercises and the worksheets became progressively more difficult.   The policy was not to deal completely with one target-area and then move on to the next, in view of the interdependence of the different capacities.   Exercises provided for the five objectives were worked at in rotation; thus we first tried to achieve a certain level of perceptual consistency and then concentrated on the observation of spatial relations.   When a certain level had been reached there we could then go on to exercises to enhance the child's mastery of perceptual consistency, etc.

1.2   The language-thought programme

The immediate objectives here were:

(a) Language development and refinement of verbal (largely oral at this stage) abilities

- learning new words and implicit concepts, development of active and passive vocabulary.

- learning morphological rules: conjugation of verbs, including reflexive verbs (including learning to use the personal pronoun); plural of nouns, etc.

- learning of syntactical rules: simple affirmative and negative sentences, active and passive sentences, compound sentences (main and subordinate clauses).

- making oneself familiar with the written language.   The intention here was by no means to teach the infants to read and write, but to prepare them for this by making them familiar with written symbols.

- knowing that something spoken can also be written and vice versa, e.g. when talking about the nice weather and the sun, the child could draw a picture of the sun on the board and write the word next to it.

- familiarity with the direction of writing (from left to right).

- general recognition of their own written Christian name.

- looking at picture-story books to arouse interest in books and to learn how books can be used (from front to back, turning the pages...).

(b) Cognitive activities and exercises

- making collections (sets): learning to gather similar elements in collections according to a particular criterion.

- working with two or more collections (sets):
Cross-classification: certain objects belong to both collection A and collection B.
Grouping: certain elements belong to collection A or B, or both.
Example: the infants are given a sheet of paper which is divided into three columns.   At the top of each column is a picture (the sky, a street, water).   The task is then to group a series of pictures of vehicles under the appropriate column.   (Grouping of the collections of carriages, vessels and aircraft).

- relations: relational concepts of place, time and proportion (bigger, smaller, warmer, colder, harder, softer...), causality.

- implications, transitivity (if A is bigger than B and B is bigger than C, then A is bigger than C).
  Example: There are pictures of toadstools on the blackboard; they are different colours and sizes; the red toadstools are big and the yellow toadstools are small. The infants answer the questions: which toadstools are big, small, red, yellow? Then there are questions like: if the toadstools are big, what colour are they?

In principle, every 'lesson' contained a series of activities centring on the point of interest which had been introduced:

- observation (question and answer, learning by discussion)

- expression (free report of experiences related to the point of interest, including expression of whatever had been experienced during observation; repeating it in one's own words).

- specific cognitive exercises or learning particular linguistic structures, frequently in the form of games.
  Example: Learning degrees of comparison by means of personification games: some infants are trees in the woods (John is the tallest tree, Mary is the smallest tree, Peter is bigger than Mary's tree and smaller than John's tree). Other infants are birds (Nancy flies faster than Dirk...). A third group collects chestnuts and leaves (a chestnut is heavier than a leaf...) etc.

2. Application

The population in question consisted of the children of unskilled (SES I) and semi-skilled (SES II) labourers.* A sociographic index card was compiled for each child attending municipal nursery schools.

On the basis of these data, two random samples were set up:

Group A consisted of 48 children born in 1966 (SES I and II), of whom 24 constituted the control group and 24 the experimental group, who began the compensation programme in the school year 1970-71 lasting until May 1972.

Group B consisted of 48 children born in 1967 (SES I and II), of whom 24 constituted the control group and 24 (the experimental group) began a replication of the programme from November 1971 until May 1973 (2).

The programme was put into practice by pre-school teachers (one for group A, one for group B) affiliated to the laboratory, and lasted over 16 to 20 weeks of each school year:

Group A: from November 1970 until April 1971
         from November 1971 until April 1972

Group B: from November 1971 until April 1972
         from November 1972 until April 1973

---

*These correspond roughly to Social Groups IV and V of the Registrar General's classification (U.K.)

The children in the experimental groups followed the programme in 'clusters' (in principle, a small group of six infants all from the same school).   For this purpose, the children were taken from the class and put in a separate room, to take part in the group activities set out in the programme.   Individual treatment was only given when a particular child was clearly hindering the progress of the group, or when he had been absent for a relatively long period.   The control groups were taken from the same schools and classes and followed the customary programme.

The original plan was to devote half an hour each day to giving each 'cluster' perceptual-motor exercises, and half an hour for speech-thought exercises. However, this proved to be impracticable, given the distance between the schools to be visited by one pre-school teacher each day.   In the end, the compensatory programme was applied to each 'cluster' on two half-days (one in the morning, one in the afternoon) each week.   The total time spent on both parts of the programme remained as originally planned.   Information about the aims of the experiment was given to the parents of the children involved (by means of home visits) as well as to the teachers and governing bodies of the classes and schools involved.

3. Evaluation

All that remains to be discussed is the evaluation.   Was the programme effective or not?

To begin with the criteria of evaluation.   The scheme provided for pre- and post-tests for each school year.   Thus, for each child we have the test results taken at four periods (at the beginning and end of each of the two programme sessions). For the perceptual-motor programme we have the Frostig Developmental Test of Visual Perception at our disposal.   This test was specially designed to test the effect of the corresponding perceptual-motor compensation programme.   It consists of five sub-tests which correspond to different components of the programme.   In addition, we used a number of sub-tests from the AKIT (Amsterdamse Kinderintelligentietest - Amsterdam Child IQ test), notably: verbal fluency, visual memory, learning names, exclusion, quantity and word-meaning.   Finally, as a general criterion of non-verbal ability we used the Leiter International Performance Scale (3).

A description of the general results of the evaluation follows (4).

3.1 The Leiter (see Table 1)

All groups (experimental and control) exhibit continuous improvement in their performances on the Leiter Scale (raw scores).   There seems to be evidence of fairly parallel progress between the experimental and control groups; it would seem that the programme has had little effect on non-verbal ability as measured by the Leiter scale.   What is noticeable is that, during the vacation period (which comes between the second and third tests) the progress of the control group is much less steep than that of the experimental group.   Although this is not a statistically significant difference, but merely a trend, it can nonetheless be indicative of Jensen's interpretation of the relation between intelligence and that which is learned systematically.   'Intelligence thus can be thought of psycho-logically as that aspect of mental ability which consolidates learning and exper-ience in an integrated, organised way, relating it to past learning and encoding it in ways that permit its retrieval in relevant new situations.   The products of learning become an aspect of intelligence (or are correlates of intelligence) only when they are organised and retrievable, generalisable and transferable to new problem situations.' (5)

It is possible that a similar form of integration of the educational material of the compensatory programme occurred in the experimental group, and that this integration requires more time, which would explain why this effect was only noticeable after the vacation.   We should, however, add that even if the advances in level of intelligence in the case of the experimental group in October had been genuine, the difference faded with time.

3.2 AKIT (see Table 2)

In the AKIT tests too, continuous progress in performance is noticeable in the four individual groups.   In contrast to what we observed in the Leiter, the differences between the experimental and the control group are most marked in the post-tests (2 and 4) immediately following the conclusion of each part of the programme.   The differences observed at the end of the first year, in which the experimental group A in particular seems to have the lead, have all but completely disappeared after the summer vacation.   At the end of the second year, the experimental and control groups diverge increasingly, but to a lesser extent than at the close of the first year of the compensatory programme.   A possible explanation may be found in the hypothesis that the compensatory programme only succeeded in bringing the infants to a level of development which they would in any case have attained a few months later.   Given, however, the stagnation in group A (experimental) during the vacation, this would not mean that the gain is cumulative, at least not after its systematic influence has disappeared.   The fact that the compensatory programme was most effective when it was first applied (first year of group A - from November 1970 until April 1971) could, among other things, be imputed to the greater initial enthusiasm, not only of the team members, but also of the schools and the parents, who received more guidance in that first year.

3.3 Frostig (see Table 3)

The most striking feature in the table of development based on Frostig's criteria is that the performances of all groups improved throughout the school year, but stagnated or even dropped (in 3 of the 4 groups) during the vacation.   This phenomenon is also mentioned by Jensen in relation to most 'scholastic achievement scores', and apparently occurs most frequently in the case of skills which must be learned and remembered systematically and which are less dependent on general intelligence - such as spelling, grammar, mechanical rules for counting, etc. The extremely specific nature of this Frostig criterion (which could be regarded as a test of school achievement) might account for the lapse during the vacation. Here too, as in the case of AKIT, we see that the programme is most effective after the first year of application in group A.

4. Conclusion

The compensatory programme was applied and evaluated twice in two years.   On the basis of the results we can conclude that the programme brought about a number of definite changes.   However,

(i)   the effects were specific, i.e. most noticeable in the criteria most closely linked with the programme activities (Frostig);

(ii)   there is no indication whatsoever as to the permanence of the results obtained, i.e. as to whether they would promote school achievements later: the gains in the experimental groups disappeared after the vacation period and there were no significant effects carried over to the Leiter test - i.e. there seems to have been no transfer effect.   Sound general ability tests like the Leiter, which specifically try to be as little sensitive to environment as possible, probably are an extremely difficult criterion in the evaluation of compensatory and enrichment programmes.

(iii) the effects of the programme proved to be time-bound: more effective in group A than group B, more effective after the first year than after the second.

NOTES AND REFERENCES

(1) Frostig, M. et al., <u>Developmental Test of Visual Perception</u>, Consulting Psychological Press, California, 1963.

Frostig, M., <u>The Developmental Program in Visual Perception, Advanced Pictures and Patterns, Teacher's Guide</u>, Follet Publishing Co., Chicago, 1967.

(2) The selection of representative samples for experimental versus control groups is generally achieved by means of random sampling. This was not possible here, for practical reasons. Thus the number of schools from which the children were drawn had to be kept to a minimum, because this would otherwise have made working with groups impossible practically. The random selection of clusters was used as a compromise. The clusters were made up of groups of six children who all met the following criteria:

(i) all at the same school (schools which were too small or which had a very low percentage of SES I or II children were excluded);

(ii) all belonging to SES I or II (a ratio of 3/3 within the cluster was aimed at);

(iii) all born either in 1966 (group A) or 1967 (group B).

In this way, 15 clusters were formed for both group A and group B, by making a random selection of children meeting the three criteria. Each time, 8 clusters were chosen at random from each set of 15 clusters, after which, again at random, 4 clusters were assigned to the experimental group (to which the compensatory programme was applied) and 4 were assigned to the control group (which was thus following the routine pre-school programme).

(3) A number of other specific criteria was introduced, such as the Utrechtse Taalniveau Test (Utrecht Speech-level test) as well as a number of personality variables as a scale for evaluating self-image and anxiety levels. A discussion of these results is not relevant here.

(4) We used a double multivariate analysis of variance. The two independent variables were, respectively, SES I vs. SES II, and experimental vs. control group. In the discussion here, the first-mentioned independent variable has not been taken into consideration; neither the 'main effects' nor the 'interaction effect' was significant.

(5) Jensen, A.R. (1973) <u>Educability and Group Differences</u>, Methuen & Co., London, p.89.

TABLE 1

LEITER Table of Development

	group A		group B	
1. Pretest 1st year	E	12.60	E	11.42
	C	12.00	C	11.17
2. Posttest after 1st year	E	16.00	E	15.30
	C	15.27	C	14.52
3. Pretest 2nd year	E	17.72	E	17.21
	C	16.24	C	15.10
4. Posttest after 2nd year	E	21.25	E	19.47
	C	20.16	C	20.31

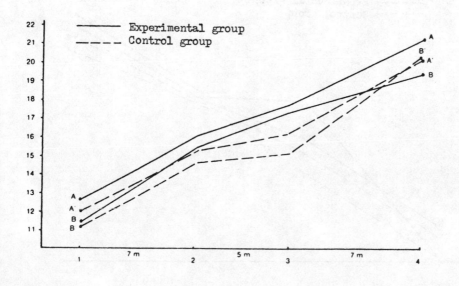

TABLE 2   AKIT Table of Development
(Average of 6
sub-test scores)

		group A		Group B	
1.	Pretest 1st year	E	7.38	E	9.01
		C	7.29	C	8.40
2.	Posttest after 1st year	E	15.63	E	13.61
		C	11.83	C	12.90
3.	Pretest 2nd year	E	15.92	E	15.52
		C	15.30	C	15.32
4.	Posttest after 2nd year	E	20.37	E	19.78
		C	18.33	C	19.05

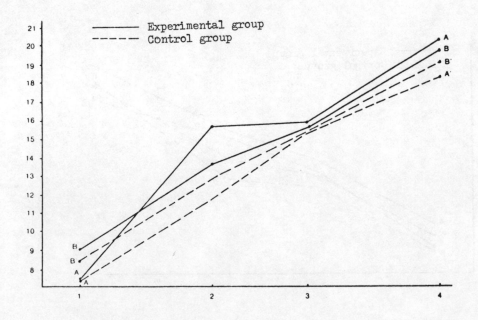

TABLE 3   FROSTIG Table of Development
(average of 5
sub-test scores)

			Group A		Group B
1.	Pretest 1st year	E	4.39	E	4.05
		C	4.76	C	4.43
2.	Posttest after 1st year	E	9.95	E	7.31
		C	7.53	C	6.74
3.	Pretest 2nd year	E	9.50	E	6.71
		C	8.18	C	6.48
4.	Posttest after 2nd year	E	11.54	E	8.67
		C	9.62	C	7.87

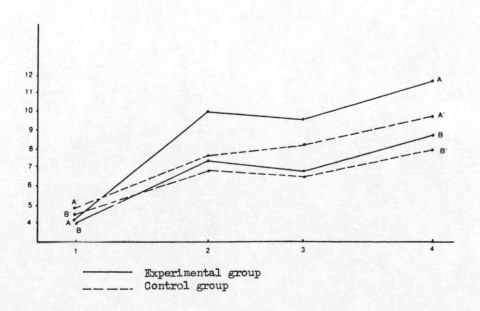

——————— Experimental group
— — — — Control group

2 The Environment. Environmental Investigation at Pre-School Level

In the preceding chapter, the team's priorities were expressed in very general terms; action to minimise retardation in working-class children constituted the principal objective. For this purpose we studied the literature relating to programmes used abroad. With some adjustment, these were applied to the second and third pre-school classes. Our treatment does not investigate the causes of developmental problems in schools, but it does arrive at a series of probable symptoms, which could be expected to exert a direct influence on school performance and which, because of their cumulative effect, in turn cause further retardation. The characteristics of socially deprived children, however, are not known. As well as an evaluation of the programme, we tried to gain insight into the environmental variables which give rise to the poor educational achievement of children from lower social levels.

1. Population and Variables

1.1 Population

In chapter 1 we described the population from which our random sample was chosen. The compensatory programme was carried out with two groups over two-year periods. Each year a pre- and post-test was applied to each group with the result that we now have at our disposal the results of four testings. By the same method as we originally composed the sample for the experimental and control groups from social classes I and II, we expanded the control group to include the higher social levels. Four social levels were thus represented in the control group. The total group was constituted as follows:

	Table 1		Table 2
	exp.	control	control
level I	24	24	19
level II	24	24	21
level III	-	24	18
level IV	-	24	21
Total	48	96	79

144

However, although when the environmental investigation began, 141 families had been included, we were able to make an environmental study of only 131 cases. The acoount of the research deals with the results of this total group whenever the discussion is limited to environmental variables; the moment the environmental variables are related to the test results, we restricted ourselves to the control group.

Finally there is a discussion of the significance of environmental variables in a second control group, for whom we have four sets of test results (pre- and post-test in the 2nd and 3rd class of pre-school). The figures for this group are given in Table 2.

1.2 Variables

Data on environmental variables were compiled on the basis of a semi-structured questionnaire. The survey was carried out on the mother. We felt that the mother would be able to provide the most useful information concerning these very young children, and the mother is usually easier to contact than the father. This does not mean that we did not consult him too.

We will restrict ourselves here to a general outline of the information sought.

A number of sections can be distinguished in the survey:

- socio-economic; the questions referred to the occupation and education level of the parents, and the composition of the family.
- living conditions; i.e. type of house, living space, the neighbourhood.
- toys available and the criteria determining their purchase; possibilities for outdoor play; how often the children are played with; which games the children enjoy most; the extent to which the children are taught certain activities.
- parental reactions to specific items of the child's behaviour.
- general aspects of education/upbringing in the family with particular reference to attitudes towards courtesy, aggression, sexuality and cleanliness.
- attitude to school.

The dependent variables in this research were determined by the evaluation criteria set out in chapter 1.

1.3 Variables according to social class

The global analysis of the survey aimed at locating the differences between social levels. This was done by means of x^2 tests. The analysis shows that the most pronounced differences are related to living space, the kind of neighbourhood and educational background. These differences are trivial.

Differences were also found in the variety of toys. Children from lower social groups have less access to toys like puzzles and clothes for dressing up. In addition, parents from higher social groups were found to play considerably more often with their children. Differences in learning scholastic skills were minimal.

Contrary to expectation, we found that dogmatic statements claiming that parents from lower social levels do not meet the appeals of their children for help are unfounded: however, at higher social levels there is a greater frequency of verbal response between parents and their children.

A number of items concerned with attitudes to education were included. As in the literature we consulted, these included courtesy, aggression, sexuality and cleanliness. The analysis reveals no differences in attitudes to either courtesy or aggression. There is slightly greater tolerance for deviant behaviour on the part of parents from higher social groups. Differences with regard to cleanliness are minimal. On the other hand, marked differences were found in attitudes to sexuality: the middle and higher group were clearly more tolerant of sexual expression in their children.

A certain amount of care must be taken in arriving at conclusions about parents' vocational aspirations for their children. The common desire of parents in all classes is that the child should have a better chance to get on in life, but this varies with social class. All conclusions are likely to be influenced by certain factors: ambitions were measured by taking as a starting point the kind of occupations considered desirable. Rising, falling or static aspirations were always considered from the position of the aspirant. This, however, causes problems in levels I and IV. In the case of the former, the level cannot drop further; in the latter, it cannot rise. Static aspirations in the case of level I are interpreted as falling, whereas for level IV as rising. We consider that this method is in fact too crude to measure aspirations adequately.

Generally speaking, we may say that the variability within each social class was considerable, but between social classes it often proved to be less than we had expected. These conclusions obviously refer only to the population represented in this sample.

2. Correlation Study

2.1 Methodology

For our consideration we have the environmental data and the test criteria referring to perceptual-motor co-ordination, verbal development and cognitive development of the extended group involved.

In an initial analysis, only those environmental variables with a significant correlation (0.5 level) with social class, on the one hand, and cognitive variables on the other, were considered.

Table 3 shows that the following variables comply with this condition.

Socio-economic level: occupation of the head of family, educational level of the head of family, educational level of the mother, available living space, neighbourhood, number of children.

Educational climate: available toys, contact with parents, level of parents' aspirations for the child, acceptance of infant sexuality.

There are two items which do not correlate significantly with social class, but which do so with cognitive variables: namely, the importance attributed to cleanliness, and the image the parents have of the social maturity of their child.

Certain items correlate with social class but do not correlate with cognitive variables, namely housing, frequency with which the child is played with, the extent to which remarks or prohibitions are explained, and statements concerning the expense of education ('studying is too expensive').

TABLE 3[+]   Table of Intercorrelations – Tests and Other Variables

	SES	TEST 1			TEST 2				TEST 3			TEST 4		
		FROST	AKIT	M	FROST	AKIT	LEIT	M	FROST	AKIT	M	FROST	AKIT	M
1) Sex	01	-06	-07	-06	-02	-05	-03	-03	04	-03	01	01	-03	-01
2) Marital status married/ single	04	-09	00	-05	-01	02	02	01	06	-03	02	05	0	02
3) Number of children	-22	-26	-26	-26	-17	-25	-28	-23	-14	-18	-16	-17	-18	-17
4) Father's profession		32	37	35	13	42	46	34	13	16	15	12	25	19
5) Father's educational level	88	34	39	36	13	41	44	33	14	16	15	15	25	20
6) Mother's educational level	77	33	34	34	12	38	42	31	17	11	12	17	25	21
7) Number of 'day rooms'*	-09	12	-09	02	-01	-09	-19	-10	07	04	01	-	-	-
8) Number of bedrooms	-32	-16	-27	-22	-07	-26	-26	-20	-05	-12	-08	-06	-14	-10
9) Global accommodation quota	-33	-18	-27	-23	-11	-28	-26	-22	-10	-15	-13	-09	-12	-10
10) Accommodation	43	05	13	09	-02	11	08	06	-08	-02	-05	-06	05	-01
11) Neighbourhood	63	27	31	29	07	34	27	23	09	18	14	09	26	18
12) Integration	03	01	-03	-01	06	01	03	03	13	01	07	08	-03	03
13) Children's toys	31	31	36	34	38	32	52	40	34	31	33	35	33	34
14) Do you play with your child?	-26	-17	-17	-17	-12	-15	-16	-14	-11	-08	-01	-20	-11	-15
15) Learned activities	-10	14	06	10	21	-03	18	12	18	14	16	24	11	18
16) Available time	15	21	25	23	16	20	30	22	14	13	14	12	20	16
17) "	01	16	07	12	20	05	06	10	16	08	12	16	09	17
18) Explanation upon making observation	29	03	18	11	04	17	17	13	0	02	01	12	14	13
19) Asking questions	03	00	14	07	07	13	08	10	19	09	14	08	14	11
20) Importance of stimuli	24	25	27	26	21	20	34	25	18	18	18	07	13	10
21) Social maturity	06	20	24	22	22	22	28	24	14	23	19	08	17	13

*rooms other than bedrooms

	SES	TEST 1			TEST 2				TEST 3			TEST 4		
		FROST	AKIT	M	FROST	AKIT	LEIT	M	FROST	AKIT	M	FROST	AKIT	M
22) Courtesy	08	04	11	07	03	13	06	08	10	09	10	09	10	09
23) Aggression	19	06	-09	-01	-00	-19	-06	-06	15	04	09	02	01	02
24) Sexuality	-39	-17	-25	-21	-16	-30	-31	-25	-12	-14	-13	-05	-18	-12
25) Cleanliness	14	19	18	19	19	16	40	25	21	18	10	18	27	22
26) Aspirations	53	22	27	25	20	32	39	30	13	12	12	11	22	17
27) Importance of study for profession	-11	-09	-08	-09	-07	-12	0	-06	-04	-10	-01	-15	-06	-11
28) Aspirations for further study	14	15	13	14	12	09	25	15	08	-04	02	0	07	03
29) Profession; respect	09	02	02	02	-02	-04	-05	-04	-01	04	02	-C7	02	-02
30) Studying too expensive	22	05	16	11	02	06	09	23	-02	01	0	-08	06	-01
31) Study interesting	02	19	05	12	-04	-02	01	-02	-01	-01	-01	05	03	04
32) Information for strangers	03	12	09	09	19	06	11	12	16	13	15	09	11	10

[+] A number which is underlined indicates a significant (p = .05) correlation
(All numbers were multiplied by 100)

2.2 Conclusions of correlation study

From the table of correlations, the following can be derived:

(i)   On average the importance of various environmental variables diminishes with age.

(ii) Amongst the environmental variables which appear to correlate with the test results, we have found some which correlate with the social class to which the parents belong. We are concerned here mainly with the educational level of the parents, which is closely associated with their occupational status; with the available living space which is obviously related to family income; and with the kind of house and the neighbourhood in which the family lives.

(iii) Other environmental variables which correlate with the test results are less easy to interpret as pure correlates of the family's social class. Here we are thinking of the kind of toys available to the child, how often the parents play with the child, how much time is set aside for the child, how much store is set by encouragement of positive attitudes. Such variables can be approached as features of the strictly educational situation of the child almost independently of social class.

(iv) Parental judgement of a child's social maturity seems to refer less to the nature of the education given at home than to a fairly satisfactory judgement of the child.

(v)   Aspirations seem to correlate strongly with social class, and although there is less correlation with the test results, they still remain a significant factor. It is curious too that the statement 'letting children study is too expensive', which correlated with SES, does not correlate with the test results. Probably the correlation with SES is limited by the strictly technical point: the answers are too obliquely dispersed and the distribution is not normal.

(vi) It is equally important to consider those items which are not correlated with test results - one of these is 'integration into the neighbourhood'. We know that some authors (Klein, Bott) regard integration or non-integration into the neighbourhood as a factor which helps to explain school success. If a given social problem can be partly explained as the result of culture clash, then we can expect an intensification of this divergence in working-class neighbourhoods where there is strong integration. This point of view is not confirmed by our findings, but

a) the coefficient of integration is derived from the number of neighbours whose occupations could be stated by the testees;

b) the way in which our sample was set up is such that it is not fully representative of all the variables of the neighbourhood in which the testees live.

Finally, whether or not parents actually teach their children(rhymes,counting,etc) does not seem to correlate with either SES or with the test variables. This variable is nevertheless important in the fourth testing in relation to a number of extremely specific criteria (Frostig 2, 3 and 4).

The nature of this item itself makes it understandable that it should not discriminate in the first testing: the children are four years old, primary school is still a long way ahead. It is curious therefore that whether or not activities are taught is related only to the Frostig, which is a perceptual-motor test.

The attitudes which the parents assumed towards their children's questions was, contrary to our expectations, not related to either SES or the test results, at least with regard to the correlations with the test results.   Items related to the extent that parents explain requests and reprimands to their children, are clearly related to social class, but not to the test results.   In the case of the AKIT criterion, the correlation would appear to reach the threshold of significance. Although this result must be considered with extreme circumspection, it is in keeping with our intuition.   If prohibitions and commands are explained to the child, then this occurs by means of speech structures.   Various authors have pointed out the importance of speech as a mediator in the impositions of rules as opposed to strictly situational commands or prohibitions.

It would thus seem conceivable that the learning effect associated with this has a greater transfer value and is expressed mainly by means of a verbal factor.   The relation is, however, much weaker than expected.   Nor does the attitude towards aggression seem to be related to the test results.   There would appear to be a connection with social class; and this is in line with other research findings. The relation is, however, weaker than anticipated; but it does tally with the observations of a number of authors who indicate that there is a trend in all social classes towards a higher tolerance of aggressive behaviour (Bronfenbrenner). Attitudes towards cleanliness have a very weak correlation with test results and none whatsoever with SES.   To our surprise, however, opinions expressed concerning the importance of the school - the desire for further study, the importance of the school for one's later career - turned out to bear no relation to the test results. Only the item concerned with the financial burden of education was related to social class, but, at the same time, it was unrelated to success at school.

(vii)   The number of children in the family appears to be negatively correlated with the test results.   This negative correlation is most noticeable in the verbal sub-tests.   One could reasonably suppose that diminished direct inter-action with the parents gives rise to slower verbal development.   The correlation with Utant rises to .52 in the first testing, but disappears in the fourth testing.

3.   Environmental Variables in relation to Test Variables: Further Analysis

3.1   Introduction

In interpreting correlational research, problems arise; cause and effect are difficult to differentiate; correlations may be caused by a variety of unconsider-ed factors.

Despite information about the extent of inter-correlations, revealed by study of the correlation matrix, what is represented in the tables cannot be fully under-stood without some attempt to classify the variables and to do so by use of factor analysis.

The strategy adopted for use in our research may be described as follows:

(a)   extraction of a number of new environmental factors from the environmental variables;

(b)   factor analysis of the test results;

(c)   relating the new environmental variables to the test variables.

3.1.1   The environmental data

To improve the reliability of individual items by grouping them, and to reveal underlying variables, we conducted a factor analysis on the items from Table 3 and arrived at a re-classification of a number of variables.   The compound

variables were labelled on the basis of the content of the component items.   The
variables considered (items refer to Table 3) are:

(1) Social class (SES) ; items 4, 5, 6, 11.

(2) Child directedness : items 13, 14, 15, 16, 17 and 19

(3) Living space : items 8 and 9

(4) Number of children : item 3

(5) Importance attached to providing stimuli for children : item 20

(6) Sexuality : item 24

3.1.2 Factor analysis of the test results

A factor analysis of the test results carried out for each item revealed that
the factor structure varied somewhat with the age of the children, particularly
in the exclusion subtest Akit 4.

The test results show greater diversity before a lengthy holiday period than
after one.   This is consistent with the view that intelligence is a consolidation
of what has been learned (both incidentally and systematically).

Although we feel safe in assuming that the factorial structure of a number of
cognitive tests remains constant, we must nonetheless approach this conclusion
carefully: the number of subjects was relatively small.

The division between Frostig and Akit was retained for the further analysis on
the basis of the factor matrices obtained before rotation.

Furthermore, we differentiated only one verbal score: namely, the total of the
standard scores of Akit 0, 3 and 7.   In the case of the pre- and post-test of
the second year it should be remembered that Akit 4 actually belongs to this
'cluster'.   We did not take Akit 4 into consideration because we felt that
comparison of the four points-of-time tests would suffer by it.

In short: we took into consideration one Akit criterion, which included the
total of the standard scores of the 6 subtests; the Frostig criterion, with the
total of the standard scores of the Frostig subtests; and a verbal score, the
total of the standard scores of Akit 0, 3 and 7.

3.2 Environmental variables in relation to test variables

3.2.1 Methodology

In our analysis we used a method somewhere between a 'predictive' and an
'explanatory' use of the regression analysis.   We performed a further analysis
in which three of the variables considered (social class, stimulus and child
directedness) were thought to exert a direct influence on the test variables.
The correlation of 'Attitude to sexuality' and 'number of children' with the test
results was felt to be spurious.

3.2.2 Summary of the results

(i) Environmental variables and Frostig

If we take the multiple correlation coefficient of the five environmental
variables with the Frostig as a measure of the influence of environment on these

test results, we notice that this influence declines throughout the different tests. It was felt that this decline might be due to a lack of discrimination in a number of items, resulting in an insufficient differentiation in the scores. The standard deviation for the different subtests and for the tests as wholes, however, proved to be fairly stable.

A comparison of the models for the different tests reveals that in the case of the younger age-group, the 'social class' variable still exercises the most important direct effect. In the other applications (pre- and post-test of the second year) the variable 'child directedness' would appear to be the variable which by far exerts the greatest direct effect on the test variable. In the first post-test, the variable 'stimulus' is also important, but it diminishes greatly in the tests of the second year.

(ii)   Environmental variables according to Akit

During the first year, the direct effect of social class according to the Akit test results, turned out to be by far the most important. It can thus be said that we have not succeeded in explaining the association between social class and the test results in terms of the intermediate variables.

Contrary to the first year, the relation between social class and the test result can, in the case of the second pre- and post-test, be partly explained by other environmental variables, and more specifically by the variable 'child directedness'. The direct effect of both variables (social class vs. child directedness) has equal magnitude. It must be remembered however, that the 'social class' variable, in the first tests, accounts for a more important part of the total variance than was the case in the two later tests. The simple correlation coefficients of 'social class' with the consecutive Akit-scores are, respectively: .54, .57, .30, .35. The correlations of child directedness with the test scores fluctuate, in all four tests, around .30. In view of the fact that we know that intelligence scores are generally more valid for five-year olds than for 4-year olds, one would perhaps not be unjustified in interpreting the scores in the first tests as being more culture-bound, although we must point out that none of the variables recorded indicates this.

(iii)   Environmental variables according to the 'verbal factor'

An analysis of the models related to the verbal scores reveals the most curious phenomenon to be the importance of the relation between tolerance and sexuality. This factor is mainly significant in the first two testings.

This finding, however, could be caused by some outside influence; it was, after all, noted that the content of what we termed 'verbal test scores' changes throughout the various tests. Whereas initially the verbal factor principally referred to verbal fluency, in the last tests, the content assumes greater complexity. Our hypothesis is that the importance of what we termed the sexuality factor is chiefly related to vocabulary and verbal fluency. This is substantiated by the relation between environmental variables and the Utant, which is a test principally concerned with the examination of simple grammatical rules (plurals, etc.). Although this test was only used in the fourth testing, the relation between environmental variables and this test reveals a great similarity to those of the verbal factor in the first two testings. It can thus be supposed that the relation is fairly reliable, but we have yet to understand it fully.

More could be discovered as to the nature of these variables if one were to examine the intercorrelation with other environmental factors. In this connection the variables SES and 'child directedness' appear to show the greatest

degree of correlation - respectively .40 and .32.   Similarly, one could refer
back to the factor analysis of environmental variables, which shows that the sex
of the child is a variable which is not highly saturated in any single factor, but
which does have a .30 saturation in various factors.

We were thus not able to specify this variable throughout our analysis.   It is
possible that the variable is indicative of the nature of the relationships, the
extent to which the children are spoken to informally, but this is mere conjecture.
M. Deutch and Whiteman had a variable which reflected the frequency of conver-
sations at meal times, and which in this respect corresponded to the pattern of
the sex variable.

4. Conclusion

We are well aware that the relation between social class and cognitive development
is hard to define.   The assumption on which our entire investigation is founded
is that the way of life of people on lower social levels differs from that of
people on higher social levels, and this gives rise to a divergence of cultural
patterns.   Empirical investigation remains a difficulty, mainly because of the
countless variables which can be found and which correlate with social class.
The bulk of conclusions concerning the significance of environmental factors in
relation to the development and continuation of the social problem are the result
of research relying on questionnaires.   The questionnaire compiled by this team
contains a variety of items drawn from similar investigations by others and only
includes those which, at one stage or another, have proved to be important for a
sound understanding of the social problem.   However, the answers from different
social groups provided us with an unexpectedly small number of items which
differentiated the social classes.   Only those items which could be directly
related to significantly lower incomes of people at an inferior social level were
clearly discriminant, e.g. accommodation, neighbourhood, and so on.   Items
referring to educational customs showed much less divergence; this trend has also
been noted in the USA and Great Britain over the past decades.

We adopted an exploratory approach to the study of the significance of environmental variables for cognitive development.   Firstly, various relevant items or
groups of items were correlated both with social class and with the test results.
Items which revealed a significant correlation with both elements were retained
for a final investigation.

A number of items which showed significant correlation to only one of the two
basic variables were added.   The major problem facing an investigation of this
kind is the relatively high degree of intercorrelation between different variables.
By using a factor analytic investigation we attempted to classify the variables in
larger groups.   The variables retained (obviously limited in number) were then
further correlated.   This final analysis revealed that the global effect of
environmental variables on the test variables (it should not be forgotten that we
are dealing here with variables occurring outside the school context) diminishes
as the child grows older.   The various test variables retained on each occasion
showed a somewhat different connection with the environmental variables considered.
In this context, the variable 'child directedness', even if the influence of social
class is removed, proves to have the greatest importance.

In the following chapter we will describe a similar investigation into the first
year of primary education.

3 Environmental Investigation at Primary School Level

1. Population and Variables

1.1 Population and sampling

The population is that of all the children in the city of Ghent liable to enter compulsory education for the first time. Thirty first-year children were selected at random. Two tests were applied to the entire sample; information concerning the environment was obtained by means of a questionnaire which was given to the parents of roughly half of the pupils participating in the investigation.

1.2 Dependent variables

At the beginning of the academic year, the PMA test (Primary Mental Abilities, Louvain version by L. Knops, 1967) was given, and at the end of the academic year we gave a Reading Comprehension test as a measure of school achievement. The four subtests of the PMA revealed a linear relation with social class; the greatest divergences were found in the verbal subtests ($R^2 = .22$). In the Reading Comprehension test the differences were also marked ($R^2 = .23$).

TABLE 4   Pre-Test: Scores for PMA

Social Class	Verbal Factor	Perceptual Factor	Quantitative Factor	Spatial Factor	Verbal and Quantitative Factor
I	17.97	15.38	11.62	10.01	28.99
II	21.94	18.01	14.03	11.51	39.97
III	23.74	19.39	16.30	13.07	40.04
IV	26.07	20.75	17.36	14.64	43.42
TOTAL	22.52	18.59	15.03	12.53	37.67
	$R = .47$	$R = .28$	$R = .31$	$R = .31$	$R = .43$
	$R^2 = .22$	$R^2 = .08$	$R^2 = .10$	$R^2 = .09$	$R^2 = .18$

TABLE 5   Post-Test: Scores for the Reading Comprehension Test

Social Class	Reading Comprehension
I	13.06
II	20.87
III	31.49
IV	40.12
TOTAL	27.33

$$R = .48$$
$$R^2 = .23$$

1.3   The independent variables: environmental investigation

Mothers were asked to complete a questionnaire.   There were two forms - A and B.

Form B was given to all parents involved in the research.   In addition and at the same time, many items of the Likert type, a number of sociological questions and the researcher's assessment were included.   In form A a number of additional items was included, with a view to defining the nature of the relation between the parents, the neighbourhood, possible difficulties in the children's upbringing, attitude towards the school, educational background, the level of aspiration of the parents with regard to the children, and the literacy levels of the parents.

We shall first discuss the relation between these variables and social stratification.   In paragraph 2 the variables established by means of the Likert scale are discussed.

Four social classes were again distinguished according to parental occupation (see Chapter 1).   A considerable number of the variables proved to have a bearing on these classes.

The results tell us much about the current social problem.   For example, in the first place, we have the aspect of sharing of responsibility between the parents, at least in relation to the children's education.   It seems that in the case of the lower social classes the task of education is, in general, the responsibility of the mother.   She it is who attends to the child's education at home, and the one who contacts the school.

In the case of the stratification variables, a number of items still show differentiation: available living space, life style, whether or not accommodation is privately owned are some of the items which can have possible repercussions on education and school results.   Unskilled and semi-skilled labourers are more frequently obliged to change jobs, and this forces them into greater occupational mobility.   We found no evidence for the view that the working-class neighbourhood is highly integrated.   A relatively large number of working-class families do not stay at one address for more than three years, and will have moved house at least once in the previous five years.

A considerably larger number of working-class children attended a crèche or kindergarten.   Although the situation has changed somewhat in recent years, kindergartens can have a negative effect on a child's development because of the poor educational environment they provide.   Pre-schools with crèches report that children who had attended kindergartens were more often than not problem children. The question remains whether this phenomenon is due to the crèche, to the nature of its population or to both.

There is no difference between social classes as far as the following factors are concerned: the child's problems of adaptation, reluctance to attend school, how often the child talks about school, the degree to which parents observed negative (or other) changes.

There are, however, clear differences as far as relationships with school are concerned. Working-class parents choose their child's school more on the basis of its geographical situation than according to its supposed educational quality. Such families are less well informed about the school their child attends, have much less to do with the school - whether or not this is in the context of parent-teacher evenings - and do not participate in organisations connected with the school (e.g. Parent-Teacher Associations).

A number of other differences were noted with regard to educational background. In the first place, working-class parents attach less importance to education, or rather, they feel that the child's personality will develop regardless of its education. The time devoted to the child varies slightly, mainly with reference to evenings during the week. Working-class children are seldom read to. Educational literature contains frequent references to differences in parental attitudes towards aggression and sexuality. These differences are there in our sample, but are relatively slight. There are, however, important differences related to the degree of importance attached to the stimulus provided at home; this could correspond to the relative unimportance attached to education (see above). Although the amount of money spent on playthings does not differ between the social classes, the type of playthings is markedly different. In comparison to higher social classes there is less variety of playthings in the lower social groups.

Great differences emerge with regard to parental aspirations for their children. This is perhaps due to the fact that every parent desires increased social mobility for his children. This mobility has already been assured for those employed on work of an average level.

Literacy in the home is a variable that frequently emerges as important in educational literature. It refers to a number of elements which correspond to the extent to which the child is presented with those cultural means which the school considers to be valuable: principally books. It is fairly clear that fewer books are available in working-class families and their children are less frequently read to. However, the items we introduced did not reveal these differences.

In paragraphs 2 and 3 we shall further discuss the nature of the relation between environmental variables and the test results. Forms A and B of the questionnaire are dealt with separately.

2. Environmental Investigation - Form B: Environmental Variables in relation to Test Criteria

2.1 Introduction

In this paragraph an attempt will be made to relate the information emerging from the investigation to the test variables; we will attempt, in particular, to elucidate the SES-test variables relationship.

We first classified items on the basis of a factor analysis. The most important part of the Form B environmental investigation was made up of stratification variables and variables related to broader cultural elements.

2.1.1 Social class and estimated variables

The following variables emerged from the more sociological items:

(i) variables included in the estimate of social class:
  a) social class (father's occupation, neighbourhood, accommodation, diploma and number of years father and mother attended day-school)
  b) interest in the child (based upon the observations and comments of the researcher: interest in the investigation, interest in the school and interest in the child).

(ii) additional non-component variables:
  a) level of aspiration for the children
  b) review of the mother's speech
  c) number of children
  d) age at which child attended pre-school full time.

2.1.2 Scales: attitude towards the child, the school and society

A second group of variables refers to broader cultural elements. Three scales of the Likert type were devised by way of a preliminary investigation. The first scale referred to the degree of either authoritarian or democratic parental attitude to children. The second scale tapped the attitudes of the parents to the school. Is the school regarded as an open institution in which teachers, with the support of the parents (cf. educational supportive conduct) do their utmost for the children, or is it regarded more as a closed institution to which the parents can contribute little, an institution which in fact excludes them? The variable emerging from these items was termed 'attitude to the school'.

We felt that social inequality, too, would affect the way in which the community is regarded. Consequently, we adopted a number of variables with bearing on 'attitude to the community'. Is the community seen in terms of conflict, in which different groups with contrasting interests confront one another, or is the community seen as an integrated unit?

2.2 Environmental variables in relation to reading comprehension and PMA

The environmental variables noted were related to PMA scores and reading comprehension test scores, through a regression analysis. By means of successive analyses, we attempted to determine to what degree the more immediate environmental variables – attitude towards the child, attitude towards the community, aspirations – could throw light upon the relation between social class and scores in the reading comprehension test. An examination of the correlation matrix revealed that the 'attitude towards the child', 'attitude towards the school' and 'aspiration' showed a high degree of correlation with reading comprehension. When social class was partialled out, 'aspiration' and 'attitude to school' retained their importance. The pattern for the PMA was somewhat different from that for reading comprehension, and a number of interpretational problems arose. The variable attitude to school was not affected by this, although the variables aspiration and attitude to the community and, to a lesser extent, attitude to the child, were.

The high degree of correlation with aspiration (even when social class was allowed for) was completely unexpected. It seems reasonably clear that parental aspiration is at least partly determined by the potential evident in the child.

Prior to the analysis, we tended to assume that any relation exhibited would mainly be indirect - from aspiration to test results; this would involve the assumption that the parents were ill informed as to their child's potential. This may well be erroneous. Since the investigations were conducted over a period of several months, we may well have underestimated the effect of the information provided by the school in the meantime. If the above reasoning is indeed valid, then aspiration assumes a different meaning.

We had two other variables at our disposal, which were the result of a judgement on the part of the researcher: 'interest in the <u>child</u>' and '<u>the mother's speech</u>'. The two variables were not incorporated into the analysis initially for fear of their having been too subjectively assessed. Their correlation with reading comprehension, however, turned out to be of a fairly high order, even with reference to the lower social group. The effectiveness of the second variable - 'mother's speech' - persisted when all other distal variables were allowed for. But it is important to note that this was only true for the reading comprehension test, not for the PMA.

Lastly, an attempt was made to combine the relation patterns which have bearing on reading comprehension and PMA. If we consider reading comprehension as a dependent variable, the PMA emerges as the strongest predictor. Moreover, 'mother's speech' and 'attitude to school' continue to have a direct relation. Aspiration for children, attitude to the community and attitude to the child have a direct correlation only with regard to the PMA.

The correlation with social class remains: the partial correlation still amounts to .27.

In the following paragraph we shall examine to what extent additional information can be obtained from supplementary variables from Form A.

3. <u>Environmental Investigation - Form A: Environmental Variables in relation to Test Criteria</u>

It has already been stated that we had complementary information at our disposal in respect of roughly half the sample dealt with in the questionnaires; the questionnaire for this subgroup contained more items.

This questionnaire was called the A-form. In this paragraph an attempt will be made to examine the significance of these supplementary items in relation to the connection between social stratification and school success which has as yet to be determined.

In paragraph 1 we discussed the relation between the answers given to these items and the social class to which the family belongs. Not all items were retained in the subsequent analysis. One prerequisite for the inclusion of an item or variable in the further analysis was that, in principle, it should be possible to compute the Pearson correlation with the social stratification, SES, and the test results.

The degree of intercorrelation among the various items was too low and the size of samples too small to permit classification of these variables on the basis of the factor analysis. Consequently we decided to make an a priori classification of them. The additional variables were thus taken into account per column and compared in terms of regression with the test variables.

The number of items which proved to be relevant for further analysis was, however, minimal. The following were retained:

- intolerance of aggression
- degree of importance attached to encouragement
- how often the child is read aloud to
- how often educational books or magazines are consulted
- nature of available toys
- frequency of contact with the school
- degree of emphasis placed on school achievement

Subsequently, we examined whether these variables exhibited any relation to the test variables (PMA and reading comprehension) when the variables noted in 2 were held constant.

Regression analysis was, in this case also, the tool used.   When the variables in the above list are combined with the variables noted in 2, only the variable 'degree of importance attached to encouragement' emerges at all clearly.   When the PMA and environmental data are combined, the variable 'importance of school achievement' achieves some degree of significance.   These results are obviously extremely dubious in view of the fact that they are the product of a double selection procedure.   This is the extent of our analysis of the data obtained from the form A environmental investigation.

4.   Summary and Conclusion

In this chapter we have given an account of an investigation into the relation between a number of environmental variables and school results with regard to pupils in the first year of primary school.   We had at our disposal the scores of an IQ test (PMA) and a reading comprehension test.   A marked difference was noted between the scores achieved by children from different social classes.

Our intention was to determine the precise relation between social class and school results by including variables more central to our concern.   Three Likert scales were set up - 'attitude to the child', 'attitude to the school' and 'attitude to the community'.   Lastly, the level of parents' aspirations for their children as an environmental variable was taken into consideration.   Apart from 'attitude to the community', which proved to be a less satisfactory scale as far as internal consistency was concerned, there was an extremely high degree of correlation between these variables and both the SES and the test criteria.   In view of the high degree of intercorrelation, however, we were somewhat uncertain as to how these various correlations should be interpreted.

An attempt was made to get a clearer picture by means of regression analyses. The correlation of these variables with the SES presents the main problems of interpretation.   We came to the conclusion that when social class was kept constant, a number of the variables mentioned remained important.

In relation to the reading comprehension criterion, 'attitude to the school' and 'aspiration with regard to the children' emerge as the most important variables.

A different pattern was noted in the case of the PMA: 'aspiration' in this case was also important; the scales only reflected 'attitude to the child'.   On the whole, it came as a surprise that 'attitude to the child' did not feature with regard to reading comprehension.   It should be reiterated that the items referred to here are related to the extent to which the parent-child relationship exhibits either authoritarian or democratic tendencies.

Correlation between 'attitude to the child' and 'reading comprehension', within the confines of the lower social strata, still amounts to .32. The relation is thus not accidental or an artefact of overriding class differences. The other variables, however, and particularly 'attitude to the school', emerge more noticeably as far as the reading comprehension criterion is concerned.

Two variables resulting from the research workers' observations were added to the variables mentioned above. These variables were only added after selection of the variables mentioned above in view of their supposedly subjective character. However, the variable established on the basis of the research workers' judgement of the mother's verbal fluency proved, contrary to expectations, to rel. .e to reading comprehension, even when the other variables were taken into consideration and even within the lower social group. This indicates that, by means of this variable, we detected an environmental aspect not reflected in the other variables. Oddly enough, this relation did not emerge in respect of the PMA.

Next, we attempted to combine the data by including the PMA also, as a predictor in the comparison related to reading comprehension. Once again, attitude to the school and verbal fluency were in strong evidence.

At the outset of the research discussed in this chapter, we had hoped to be able to indicate a structure in which social class would refer to wider values and norms, which would then be related to more specific characteristics; we would subsequently be able to indicate their relation to reading comprehension and/or PMA. In contrast to paragraph 2, in which a number of variables were clearly suitable for use in subsequent analysis, the specific items (form A) proved to be much less useful. There were frequent differences between the social classes, but the degree of relation of the grouped items to school results and/or PMA was not high. Nevertheless, the various items were still taken into consideration from the point of view of their presumed relevance. In compiling the questionnaire, we had been guided by explanatory theories explicit in educational literature and by existing questionnaires, such as that of the Plowden Report(1),Rupp's questionnaire(2) and others.

From the point of view of action, this chapter corroborates a number of guidelines connected with compensatory programmes. Active collaboration between both school and parents would appear to be important, both at the pre- and primary school levels. In every analysis, the degree of relation between attitude to the school and results achieved at school was fairly high. In addition, we shall also establish strategies of change related to the social problem,principally in the school but bearing in mind that the parents will have to be actively involved.

REFERENCES

(1) Plowden Report, Children and their Primary Schools, Vol.I: The Report; Vol.2: Research and Surveys. HMSO, London, 1967.

(2) Rupp, J.C.C. Opvoeding tot Schoolweerbaarheid. Wolters-Noordhoff, Groningen, 1969.

4 Transition Phase

The results of the evaluation of the compensatory programme conducted in Ghent (described in Chapter 1) tally with findings of similar work elsewhere. Programmes for this age-group, and particularly the most systematic programmes tend to yield clear gains in the post-test immediately after the programme. Such gains however are not lasting. These temporary gains may only indicate that systematic teaching will produce immediate learning, but what is unclear is the question of which aspect of the programme brings about this effect. When programmes of similar types are compared they usually show clear gains in the test scores of the experimental group, but very different (experimental) programmes do not generally reveal any great mutual difference in their general results, except in specific criteria.

It would thus seem probable that what is learned is of less relevance than the circumstances in which the learning takes place, and that the most important elements concern the nature of the infant-teacher relationship and the extent to which the teacher is aware of her objectives. These observations are based on the evaluation of compensatory programmes; and this is perhaps the most important contribution of the compensatory education movement, for it is only through evaluation that we become aware of our own prejudices and are thus able to eliminate wrong attitudes and come to provide the power for effective action. Evaluation is necessary therefore, in particular because of its function as a tool for the development of the action.
However, this presents us with a number of problems:

1. Every educational event is extremely complex. A large number of characteristics of the educational situation can influence the output. The classical experimental paradigm of the social sciences attempts to control these complexities by matching them for both the experimental and control group. This is necessary in order to examine the independent effect of the variable in question. But this does not afford us much insight into the relative importance of these different situations for the results of the programmes(1).

It is worth noting that a significant proportion of the effective American programmes has been applied in a fairly specific context, e.g. in an experimental school. Generalising from such results suffers because of this; the broader educational situation was not explicitly included. The compensatory programme applied in Ghent proved successful at the end of one year. The effects of its replication fell below expectations. We have failed to explain this phenomenon,

though we do have some suggestions to make: the replication was not conducted by
the same pre-school teacher, and less guidance was given. This need not
necessarily have had repercussions on the attitude of the pre-school teacher
herself. It could be that the other people involved were less interested, the
classrooms available less suitable, and so on. The list can obviously be
extended. The point is probably that we were dealing with two programmes made
different by the environment, the teacher's attitude, and so on, rather than with
a repetition of the basic programme.

2. In view of the complex nature of educational situations, it would seem fair
to suggest that the social sciences, as they stand now, are not able to tell
educators how to structure their work so as to eradicate the problems of retardation of children from lower socio-economic environments - always assuming that
the school is in fact able to make a significant contribution. Admittedly, a
number of promising suggestions are to be found throughout the psychological,
educational and sociological literature concerning the mechanisms of social
deprivation. But our impression is that scientists have jumped to premature
conclusions. The promises are for the most part not fulfilled. We are simply
not yet in a position to derive from established theories a strategy which is
both detailed, comprehensive and effective.

3. What has been proved is that the most effective programmes are those typified
by clear planning, by detailed definition of objectives related to abilities in
the cognitive sector. It is also true that these were the programmes evaluated
most rigorously; and the fact that there were no results in more general programmes can perhaps be attributed to the fact that inadequate evaluation criteria
were used. The point is, evaluation is essential if a decision is to be taken
on the desirability of applying a programme on a broader scale.

On first sight, this might appear to present a dilemma:

a) The current state of the scientific investigation, both evaluative or non-
   evaluative, makes the development of specific strategies desirable. For
   this evaluation to be generalisable, the school situations must be comparable.

b) Education, however, is a phenomenon of great complexity. The fact that we
   are unable at this time to define in adequate behavioural terms more extensive and inclusive objectives, and that we cannot yet differentiate between
   the operative factors in an educational situation, must not cause us to
   overlook this fact.

Educationalists have expectations of how a school should function. On what
grounds would we ask them all now to teach in the same way, so that we are able
to evaluate new programmes?

However, the prospects are not entirely as bleak as they might at first appear.

In an investigation carried out in every primary school in Ghent, our expectation
was that the teachers' educational ideologies, their conception of their
profession and of their pupils, and their preference for certain general educational strategies, would all be a function of the type of school in which they
were teaching. This did not appear to be so. There were important variations
within different aspects, but these did not differ between the group of teachers
working in working-class schools and the other groups. Nor was any differentiation noticeable between experienced and inexperienced teachers. It could
be tentatively concluded therefore, that there is relative consensus as far as
the functioning of the school is concerned. Collaboration with the teachers
involved in the pre-school project substantiated this opinion. When teachers
are brought together, the general outlines of appropriate educational situations

are soon formulated (2).

This consensus in no way implies that these characteristics have been generally realized within our educational system; nor does it imply that endeavours to attain this would not meet with opposition, for any change within an existing system brings with it a degree of uncertainty which, in view of the teachers' relatively dependent status, can have serious repercussions.

We shall now outline a number of basic features which we consider it advisable to include. In view of the fact that we have been trying to realise these principles in the class since 1974-75, we shall include some elements of this application.

1.   Importance of <u>cooperative action with the parents</u>. When the home and the school are regarded as two separate worlds by the child, educational retardation can be expected. Our own investigation revealed that the parents' attitude to the school is one of the most important indices related to the child's school achievement in his first years at school. This relation persisted when both social class and the child's IQ were kept constant (see chapter 3). How can this cooperative action with the parents be realised? A school social worker could be used, but this would call for extremely intensive work. In the context of the programme, this course of action was only considered in the case of 'problem children' in the class.

In general, an attempt was made to involve the parents in the school programme. From a mastical viewpoint, the parents are invited to:

- take an active part in the work of the classroom, e.g. the parents were invited into the class to talk to the children about the work they do;

- to accompany the class on outings;

- to exchange ideas and information during parent-teacher evenings;

- to take an interest at home in what the child does at school (by means of so-called 'home chores'), to collect material required by the programme from time to time.

2.   The learning programme at school should take the <u>children's experience as its point of departure.</u> Exploratory activities should be stimulated. This implies that the teacher's attitude towards the children should be such that the pupils will have the confidence to take the initiative. For this to happen, teachers must feel secure and an atmosphere of trust must exist between teachers and pupils. This makes new demands on the way in which teachers maintain discipline and order in the class. A punitive attitude will be likely to impede initiative on the part of the children. It seems more positive to 'explain' rules and standards and to allow the children to discover for themselves the need for such standards.

Of course this is a function of the size of the class. One of the commonest findings of compensatory programmes is that work with small groups in which there is a high ratio of adults to children is the most effective means. This is even more true for very young children.

One obvious way to increase this ratio is to introduce adults other than teachers into the class, e.g. parents or grandparents, and induce them to become actively involved in class life.

It is also important in such a work-situation to divide the children into small groups (see point 4), and the possibility of doing this is a function of size and

equipment of the classroom.   Too many pre-school teachers are obliged to work
with too many children in rooms which are too small.   Even if new classrooms
were to be constructed, the official norms have not been appropriately modified.

3.   Importance of teachers' greater awareness of their objectives and understanding of what class activities are intended to achieve.   If the teacher has
no clear purpose in mind, she cannot intervene effectively and sensitively.   Any
activity or lesson can only be assessed if its objective has been stated before-
hand.   Evaluation also implies that one has available the means of measuring the
extent to which objectives have been realised.   Coupled with this is the idea
that evaluation forms an essential aspect of any educational activity.   Chapter 1
related our attempt to assess the effectiveness of the programme by comparison of
the results of children in the experimental and control groups.   This was
termed summative evaluation.   Here we are more concerned with formative evaluation, i.e. evaluation within the programme, in which a continuing appraisal is
made of those children who succeed and those who fail.

The most important function of the formative evaluation is the way in which it
modifies the procedures.   This can assume two forms:

- in the developmental phase of the programme the results of the formative
  evaluation will aim mainly at programme feedback.   If programme activities
  appear to be ineffective, modifications will be made.   Similarly, the need to
  provide other activities to attain the desired objectives may become apparent.

- in the case of a programme which has already been devised, the steering of the
  programme on the basis of internal evaluation works in a somewhat different
  way: the assessment tests assume a diagnostic character in as much as they
  indicate which children are not exhibiting a desired behavioural change.
  These children in particular should be provided with complementary activities;
  the term 'compensation' will now be used only in this sense.

Obviously, formative evaluation is carried out continuously by the teacher, and
the educational activity is constantly realigned.   Each week the team compiles
a number of criterion referenced tests which should leave scope for comments as
to the degree objectives were realised over a period of several days.   These
criterion referenced tests in their turn help to define the objectives more
precisely.

4.   One central idea is that as many children as possible should profit from
what the class has to offer(3).   In view of the differences of experience and
potential of children in the same class, it cannot be expected that every
activity and the time allotted to it will produce the same effect on each child.
Hence, an individual approach will have to be used, by introducing alternative
activities for children who have not as yet achieved the objectives.   This
implies that children will be allowed to work together in small groups.

5.   An individual approach, introduction of compensatory activities and team
work all demand greater flexibility and creativity on the part of the pre-school
teachers involved.   Hence they feel the need to share their classroom experiences
once a week, by meeting to discuss these with an educational adviser.   In
practice, this presupposes that school inspectors assume an advisory role as
opposed to a supervisory one, and that a supernumerary teacher be assigned to
each group of pre-school teachers to make their weekly discussion sessions
possible.   Originally, we had intended this additional teacher to fill a role
aimed more at compensatory work with children.

We have already mentioned two aspects of educational organisation which can, to a
considerable degree, determine the educational climate of the classroom, and over

which we as a team have no power - namely, the number of children per classroom and the space available(4).

A third aspect deals with the possibilities of forming work areas in the classroom, which are obviously essential for group work.

A fourth aspect deals with classroom furniture, and some change was brought about in the classes which were least well equipped.

In chapter 5 we will discuss the nature of the programme developed during the academic years 1974/75 and 1975/76. We chose to deal with the elements outlined above in a separate section because that is the way they occur in two programme development strategies which were tested on a small scale.

The first application was a complete failure because the application of the programme was tested by an experienced pre-school teacher without much discussion with the classroom teacher. Understandably this resulted in strong opposition to the test procedures.

A second trial was carried out by a group of 5 pre-school teachers. Here, it proved necessary to write out the particulars of the programme in full. The principles mentioned earlier are of a too general nature to be of much practical use to the pre-school teachers. They provide no more than a framework upon which classroom practice can be based.

The further development of the programme can be discussed in terms of:

- the general educational context;
- a precise written description of day-to-day activities and their corresponding objectives;
- the development of specific aids for children who have not achieved the set objectives.

Chapter 4 gives an account of the activities carried out over the years 1974/75 and 1975/76. Particular emphasis is placed on the first two points.

Conclusion: the focal point of the compensatory action was that a number of children are unable to participate fully in formal learning. The importance attached to evaluation plays an essential part not only in determining the effectiveness of a programme, but also in determining the workable components of the programme. It is on the level of evaluation that, for the time being at least, scientific investigation has most to offer. But, regardless of how significant test results may be, the laboratory situation differs too greatly from the school situation for generalisation to be at all feasible. Notwithstanding the relevance of the literature on the problems of social deprivation, the fact remains that programme development relies to a great extent on intuition. As a consequence, we involved the teachers themselves more intensively in the development of strategies. Hence the task assigned to scientific investigation is to follow the experiments and to evaluate them.

NOTES AND REFERENCES

(1) In other words – if different educational situations could be included in
the research design as independent variables, an 'educational situation x
programme' effect on children's achievements might result.

(2) It should be noted that one of the most frequently voiced complaints was
that the (pre-)school teachers work in extreme isolation.

(3) Block, J.H. (Ed) <u>Mastery Learning, Theory and Practice</u>. Holt, Rinehart &
Winston, New York, 1971.

(4) In one investigation, six children were taken from each of a number of
classes, most of which were not part of the pre-school scheme.   This
reduced the number of children per class to roughly twenty.   The pre-school
teachers themselves were astonished at the difference this made to
conditions in the classroom: everything went so much more smoothly.

5 The Pre-school Project: Period 1974-1976

In chapter 4 an attempt was made to indicate that our main aim in the current programme was 'educational innovation'.

Subsequently, the more practical aspects of the project were described. Several points should be emphasized however, Because teachers are themselves mainly responsible for carrying out the work of the project, it is obvious that radical change is not the point at issue. On the contrary the principles quoted in chapter 4 have been common knowledge for some time. This however only refers to educational ideals. Classroom situations deviate greatly from this 'optimum', for a number of reasons: the physical infrastructure of the class and the number of children present frequently exercise an unfavourable influence; the teacher is extremely isolated, and so on.

The first phase is concerned with improving the broader educational context. The second phase incorporates the introduction of 'compensatory activities', and constitutes a major part of our activities in the academic year 1976-77 (see chapter 6).

There follows a discussion of the objectives and content of the broader programme, its application and its evaluation.

1. Objectives and Content of the Programme

In chapter 4 the main prerequisite was the teacher's understanding of and adherence to the aims of the programme. We also stated that we are not yet in a position to integrate the objectives into a specific framework of objectives. The formulation of more extensive objectives remains a somewhat arbitrary process.

By way of illustration let us consider the following objectives, set out by Brophy, Good and Nedler, 1975, page 94 (1):

- Assisting the child in mastering expressive and receptive language skills that are necessary for the development of problem-solving and thinking abilities.

- Assisting the child in the development of sensory-perceptual skills.

- Assisting the child in acquiring interpersonal skills necessary for interacting effectively with peers and adults.

- Assisting the child in acquiring interpersonal skills necessary for achieving
personal autonomy.

We quote the above objectives in view of the fact that they are typical of an
approach resulting from compensatory action.   The first three objectives are
well suited for immediate inclusion at primary school level; the last two refer
to objectives related to the socialising processes which must be established if
what is generally thought of as education is to have any chance at all of success.

Although there would not seem to be much argument over whether these objectives
should be adopted in the pre-school, there might well be argument as to whether
alternative objectives should not be adopted.   A great many people in the pre-
school will consider this set of objectives to be too limited.

Discussion on these points continues within our team, because of the difficulty
in distinguishing the objectives from the content of activities, and also because
in the pre-school, objectives more often than not do not refer to immediately
obvious behaviour (e.g. pre-school children should be allowed to use materials
for creative purposes).

As a consequence of this difficulty, the teachers are in general more inclined to
consider content rather than objectives; accordingly, the central concept of our
project is not realised as a matter of course, and the development of broader
structures of objective, even from a scientific viewpoint, is still embryonic.

In practical terms, this implies that a programme should be written down in full
detail, in terms of both content and objectives, and by way of example we compiled a year's 'frame' - a structure incorporating a number of themes, each
consisting of a series of central items.   Each central item relates to one
particular theme.   These central items (providing work for a fortnight) are
divided into a number of activities, each with a specific objective.

1.1 Year's frame

The year's frame indicates the nature of the correlation between the various
central items, and from this, a programme in which emphasis is placed on the
child's investigation of his environment, is compiled.   The first central items
stress investigation of the relation between the child and his immediate environment, with particular reference to the school and the family.   Subsequently, the
horizon is broadened.

The following diagram illustrates the succession of various central items.

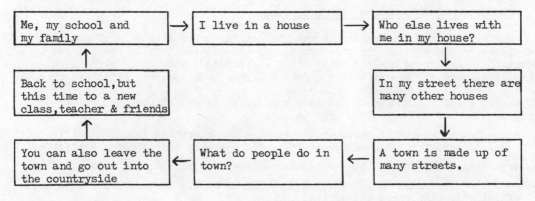

Each central item stems from the preceding one.

The first centres on the individual child (Who are you, boy, girl? What do you look like? Who is your best friend? What does he/she look like? Let's look at our reflection in the mirror together. Do we look like one another? No, you have blond hair, I have brown hair. Let's make a doll that looks a bit like us, etc.)

The following central item again centres on the individual child but brings out what the child can do. Thus 'fun and games' in the central item 'I play' leads to questions like - How do we play? Alone? Together? With what? Did mummy and daddy play when they were young? Did the headmaster play too? How did he play? Let's go and ask him. This is one way in which those responsible for the school and the parents may be closely involved in this work.

This brings us to the third central item: After school I go home; I live in a house; Johnny lives in a house too, but it looks quite different from ours. We saw this when we made that outing, etc. We'll build our own house in the classroom, with real things - wood and nails etc.

Working with the progression from one theme to another within the yearly frame has many advantages. It makes it easier for the teacher to relate activities to the general objectives. The preceding central items can, moreover, be used repeatedly (2).

The aim now is to proceed to several alternative activities, in cooperation with the class teachers. It would seem that a more extensive common frame would facilitate exchanges among the various schools.

Finally, we feel we have integrated classical 'centres of interest' into a more extensive time-span.

1.2 Global development of a central item

Each central item lasts approximately a fortnight. It brings together about 50 activities and incorporates the reason for the choice of this particular theme, a number of broad objectives (including a specimen language chart which lists the recently introduced concepts), and a number of additional activities for any group which may have failed to attain some of the objectives.

The structure of each central item comprises:
(a) an introductory phase
(b) a developmental phase
(c) an evaluative phase

(a) The introductory phase

The theme is introduced, for example, by a puppet show, a slide show, a 'talk' with the class mascot, group discussions with the infants, looking at picture-story books together, discussing photographs or pictures which the children have brought to school, and so on.

Next follow activities related to observation and experience in both the immediate and broader contexts, designed to give the infants scope to experience the topic in a group context. During this phase, the children leave the school; partic-ular stress is placed on direct experience. This can take the form of bus or tram outings; going to look at both the inside and outside of a house together; going shopping by oneself; going to the station together; going to the playing

fields, the park, the farm together, etc.   We are convinced that experiences of
this kind have a far more intense effect than classroom discussion, and the effect
is increased by participation within the group.   This ensures that subsequent
activities will in fact relate to the experience of all the children.

(b) The developmental phase includes activities aimed at affording the children
the greatest scope for integrating these experiences by means of a number of
expressive activities at individual and group level.   Songs, rhymes, stories,
gymnastic games, expressive movement are all adapted to suit the given topic.

(c) The evaluation phase

Each day commences with a discussion of the activities for that particular day,
as well as a recapitulation of the events of the preceding day; and at the end
of the day, the day's events are discussed.   The infants' work is discussed in
group context: 'what do we think of the work, can it be done differently...?'

Some criterion referenced tests are used, the results discussed and errors made
corrected in group discussion.   Finally, each central item is concluded by a
collective evaluation and by relating the item to the broader yearly frame.

1.3 Activities

Each central item is sub-divided into six activities, each dealing with a
particular aspect of the central item.   We mentioned earlier that each activity
is presented together with its corresponding objective.

Here we distinguish a number of target areas which correspond to one acceptable
classification of human behaviour: perception, language and thought, action and
movement, social relationships and personality.

(a) Perception

Some examples: acoustic discrimination of phonemes, differentiation between
figure and background, perception of rhythm, classification of objects according
to their particular features.

(b) Language and thought

It is difficult for us to differentiate between language and thought.   We differentiate between the formal and expressive aspects of language - between on the
one hand the enlargement of vocabulary, competence in grammatical structure,
stimulation of good articulation, and, on the other, communication, symbolization,
expression.

Children of the age group considered should already be able to formulate and
carry out complex verbal instructions, they must be able to speak in a group, be
able to grasp and convey information coherently.   Language for us is central.

Obviously, language cannot be dissociated from the development of thinking, and a
first series of objectives in the development of thinking is concerned with the
stimulation of concept formation.   Moreover, great emphasis is placed on
relational concepts (quantitative, qualitative, temporal and spatial).

Problem solving is equally obviously an important aspect of the thought process.
A distinction can be drawn between problems which have a particular solution
(convergent thinking) and those which involve divergent thinking.   In the first
case, for example, we set the children problem questions: if five policemen are
standing on the street corner and two of them leave, how many are left?   In the

second case, we might ask the children to think of a way of purifying water.

(c) Action and movement

A basis of knowledge is essential if a child's actions and movements are to be fully under control: experience and knowledge of the body and parts of the body, spatial orientation (knowledge of spatial concepts, both static -'in','on','under'- and dynamic -'up','down','forward') left and right spatial organisation.

Motor skills and body control: weight, respiration control, muscle relaxation, coordination of movements, motor and sensory coordination (eye-hand coordination in particular), dissociation (for example, supple arm-hand motor skills, essential in drawing and writing, depend on the rest of the body remaining relatively still).

Control and knowledge of the body, and that of the spatial environment are closely connected and mutually influential.

Learning a number of basic techniques: manipulation of pencil and paper, paint-brush, paint, scissors, books, boxes, rope, clay, building blocks, etc.

Non-verbal expression: manual, motor, musical, rhythmic expression. Learning technical skills and developing a sense of rhythm is a prerequisite for expressive work, just as the speech is a prerequisite of verbal communication and expression. However, in the case of the infant class, emphasis is placed on practical experience.

(d) Personality and social relationships

Stimulation of the desire to achieve: our main course of action here is to offer children activities which arouse their interest, and to present them with problems which demand effort on their part but which are nonetheless within their grasp, so that they are praised if they find the solution.

Stimulation of a positive self-image. Self-image is very closely connected with how the child sees himself in relation to others, particularly his teacher and friends. Consequently, apart from showing each child equal appreciation and giving everyone a chance, etc., the teacher will have to teach the children that everyone has something interesting to tell, that every child has positive and negative attributes, that 'who's best?' is not always the same person (e.g. by conducting games of chance in which everyone can alternately win or lose).

Stimulation of independence. Children must learn how to dress, wash themselves.. learn to run an errand on their own, to carry out an assignment independently, i.e. that they do not ask for help when it is not needed but, on the other hand, they ask for help if they find they cannot solve it on their own.

Learning to work in a group. Working in a group implies that the children can learn to allocate tasks amongst themselves, and stick to what they have agreed to do. This presupposes a consideration of the feelings and wishes of others, and that they can regard their peers as sources of knowledge or assistance in solving problems or carrying out assignments.

Clearly so brief an outline does not do full justice to what is being attempted. It lacks precision partly because our programme and objectives are still tentative and in course of development.

2. Application

The programme was carried out with the active cooperation of the schools of the city of Ghent, in ten classrooms (3). The basic principles described in chapter 4 of the present report were adhered to, with one exception.

2.1 Educational guidance

In the course of the transitional phase, two pre-school teachers at a time were allowed a half-day off per week, during which time their place was taken by two pre-school teachers from the Pedagogical Centre. This seemed the most satis-factory form of guidance as far as the teachers' contribution to the proposed activities was concerned, but less so for the management of classroom change.

From 1975-76 we had two pre-school teachers at our disposal. Each teacher visited 5 schools weekly, spending one entire morning or afternoon in the class. In addition, twice termly, the pre-school teachers met with the members of the team to find solutions to a number of problems which had arisen in their work.

The 'educational advisors' became the link between the team and the schools. Guidance, explanation of intentions, help and classroom demonstrations constituted one aspect of their role. Acting as a channel to pass on to the team criticisms or objections related to the programme was another.

It must be emphasised that guidance is essential to educational innovation. Even in the case of the original compensatory programmes this was undoubtedly one of the components which gave rise to gains in the post-test.

2.2 Cooperation with the parents

Chapters 2 and 3 reflect the great importance of the parents' attitudes to the school. It was thought that this cooperation would take a smoother course with the help of two activities:

(a) At home

There were frequent requests for children to bring to school scrap material from home. These 'home assignments' were not particularly time-consuming but did call for interaction with the parents. The plan met with opposition from some parents, and we finally abandoned it precisely because the very parents we most wanted to involve in school life were those who most objected to it.

(b) In school

In the first place, a parent-teacher evening was arranged at the beginning of the academic year. A certain amount of direct information was given during the evening, but the principal aim was to demonstrate a simple activity to the parents, to the governing body and to the team. We feel that this method makes it possible to indicate, in a practical way, what goes on in class and how a child learns through play.

Parent-school cooperation was also brought into the classroom itself. In the programme, and more particularly at the start of each central item, the class made regular excursions and parents were free to come along. Parents were invited to come into the class itself, mainly in connection with particular activities (e.g. traffic is being discussed - a father who is a policeman comes, in uniform, to the school and gives an account of his work; the town gets dirty, that is why the Sanitary Department is necessary, etc.).

In the future it is hoped that it will be possible to invite parents to help with other activities, e.g. mother can help a group playing with clay, father can help make the soup, etc. This will of course only be possible if definite appoint-ments are made and if parents can accept that they come to help with a class group and not with their own child. There is still a long way to go before this can be achieved.

2.3 The school social worker

We found that it was difficult to contact some parents, but because it was not possible to contact all of these individually, the social worker got in touch only with parents whose children were considered to be 'problem cases' at school.

3. Evaluation

In chapter 4 we summarized the difference between summative and formative evaluation.

With respect to formative evaluation, the team established a number of criterion referenced tests. These tests followed the programme step by step, were always, to a lesser or greater extent, specific, and contributed to the modification of the programme and to providing specific help for certain children.

We shall limit ourselves here to a brief discussion of summative evaluation which should allow us to pass judgement on the relative efficiency of the programme.

Summative evaluation is only possible by means of a comparison of an experimental and a control group. Consequently, the evaluation instruments should be less programme-bound.

3.1 Pre-test with a random group

At the beginning of the academic year, the N.S.T. (Nijmegen School Ability Test (4)) was used as a pre-test on a number of children chosen randomly from both the experimental group and the control group (5). Six children were selected randomly from each class involved in the investigation. The differences in test scores between the experimental group and the control group were not significant in any of the 10 subtests. These subtests were subjected to a factor analysis, whereby the 10 subtest scores could be combined with two global scores; the first factor indicates the perceptual-motor skills, the second factor refers more to 'memory'.

In table 3.1.1 the average scores for both the experimental group and the control group are as follows: (6)

TABLE 3.1.1

	Experimental	Control	Total
Perceptual-motor	50.25	49.83	50.00
Memory	49.83	50.34	50.00

Since there are no significant differences between the experimental and control groups, any differences noted in the post-test can be attributed to a programme effect (7).

3.2 Post-test

A post-test was carried out at the end of the academic year on both the experimental and control groups. The tests were carried out in the usual way and spanned three 45-minute sessions.

The number of sub-tests included was fairly high (8).   The results of these sub-tests were also factor analysed.   Four factors resulted.   The first refers to general non-verbal skills, the second is a speech factor, the third refers to fine motor skills, and the fourth to perception.   The average scores of the experimental group and control group (9) are given in table 3.2.1.

TABLE 3.2.1

	Experimental	Control
General skills	50.40	49.20
Speech	51.80*	46.40*
Motor skills	50.80	48.40
Perception	49.88	50.24

*statistically significant   (F-test $p < .05$)

The table indicates that the only significant difference between the experimental group and the control group is in the area of speech.   It would appear that the programme has a beneficial effect on the speech skills of the children.

The speech factor grouped the subtests 'comprehension of grammatical structures', 'vocabulary' and 'factual knowledge', i.e. subtests of the third test.

Three classes were removed from the experimental group because, for various reasons, it had not proved possible to run the programme adequately in them.   Table 3.3.1 shows the average scores of the modified experimental group and the control group, likewise after transformation (10).

TABLE 3.3.1

	Experimental	Control
General skills	51.04	48.46
Speech	52.54 *	46.18*
Motor skills	50.85	48.65
Perception	50.76	48.86

Differences related to the speech factor would appear to emerge even more clearly here;   the other scores are higher too for the experimental group than for the control group, but the differences are not statistically significant.

It can thus be concluded that the experimental programme - in the broad sense of the word - was primarily a 'speech-enrichment programme'.   This is further substantiated by the scores on the individual subtests (these are not given here).

Lastly, we examined whether there was a relation between the occupational level of the parents and the effect of the programme.   Without going into all the details, it can be said that no interaction effects were noted;   the benefit gained from the programme did not differ according to whether children came from lower or higher social levels.   There was, however, a clear relation between the achieved scores and the occupational level of parents.   The averages referring to general skills, speech, motor skills and perception are significantly higher for the children from higher social levels than for children from lower social levels.

NOTES AND REFERENCES

(1) Brophy, Good & Nedler. <u>Teaching in the Pre-school</u>. Harper & Row, New York, 1975, page 94.

(2) The fact that the central items with their practical activities are offered in written form is not meant to impede the spontaneity or creativity of the pre-school teacher; they are intended to be a source of support and reference. Obviously the programme must not stand in the way of other classroom activities.

(3) For the academic year 1975/76, all pre-school teachers taking part in the project were from the municipal educational service. Three teachers were assigned to the team to guide their colleagues in class and to write programmes of activity.

(4) Mönks, F. et al., <u>Nijmeegse Schoolbekwaamheids Test</u>, Berkhout, Nijmegen, 1969.

(5) The aim of this evaluation was to examine whether classes involved in the experimental programme exhibited gains in comparison to classes not involved.

(6) A linear transformation was applied to the factor scores, with the result that the average score of the entire group is 50 and the standard deviation is 15.

(7) Throughout this global evaluation, the question remains as to what the term 'programme' actually implies. In this instance does it imply the programme sensu stricto?, the guidance? the cooperation with the parents? or a combination of all these components? We cannot answer this question; nor do we feel it is important to do so in the context of this scheme. We attempted to optimize the broader educational situation, a procedure which cannot be completed in one year; for it is in fact never finished. The evaluation of more specific 'compensatory strategies' on the other hand can be incorporated into an experimental context to a far greater extent; consequently a more satisfactory explanation of its 'operative components' can be provided.

(8) The following is a list of the subtests included within the various tests:
   <u>Test 1</u>: quantitative concepts, problem questions, memory, concrete likenesses, ticking off matching letters, ticking off matching words, function of symbols.
   <u>Test 2</u>: spatial orientation, shape-background discrimination, taking geometrical shapes out of a context, mazes, copying a shape joined by dots, copying a drawing, pointing out an absurdity in a drawing, completing a drawing of an object, copying abstract shapes.
   <u>Test 3</u>: negative sentences, active sentences, passive sentences, time, vocabulary, factual knowledge, stories.

(9) A linear transformation was also applied in this case to the factor scores; with an average of 50 and a standard deviation of 15.

(10) It might come as something of a surprise that the average scores for the control group are different in each table, although the same group is in question.   This is, however, a result of the fact that the random sample average was set at 50 in both cases.   In view of the fact that the experimental group's average score increases after the three classes mentioned before were extracted, there is a relative decrease in the case of the control group.   It should also be noted that the omission of three unsatisfactory experimental classes does not affect the pre-test scores so far as initial differences are concerned.   Experimental and control groups do not significantly differ.

6 Integration of Pre-school Project and Compensation Project

During the period of the project's funding by the Bernhard Van Leer Foundation, the University team and the city of Ghent cooperated increasingly in the work with pre-school children. When this phase came to an end, the city of Ghent made it possible for the project to continue, and this chapter describes its activities from 1976 until 1978.

1. The Basic Curriculum

A prerequisite of the broad based programme was that it should develop from being a 'list of prescribed daily exercises' to a 'valuable source of information' for the teacher. Consequently, the programme was applied in a less rigid manner; both the educational advisors and the teachers were free to put forward alternative activities, and provide us with details of both the activity and its objective. The only restriction was that the nature of the activity should remain the same. In this way an 'activities bank' was gradually developed.

Particular attention was given to two basic principles of the programme which had not previously been given sufficient attention, namely cooperation with the parents and group work in the classroom. The latter was indispensable in situations involving heterogeneous groups and allowing the provision of extra help for the weaker group. In this way, it is possible to differentiate between pupils and introduce individualised activities. We considered cooperation with the parents of prime importance, though this still presents some difficulties.

Development of the programme starting from 1970 could be concisely sketched as follows. Subsequent to an initial period in which our primary concern was the development, extension and evaluation of compensatory activities outside the specific classroom situation, we progressed to a new teaching system which took shape gradually. We attempted to invest the word 'compensation' with a much wider meaning: 'help given to children who have failed to achieve set objectives'. The lack of extensive means of assistance was sorely felt. Consequently we decided to experiment with specific activities of short duration.

2. Specific Programmes

2.1 Introduction

Clearly, although the final evaluation revealed that the experimental group was well ahead of the control group in terms of achievement, a number of children still had not mastered the basic skills sufficiently to begin their primary education on a sound footing.   This finding is a springboard for much initiative.   To begin with, one must take into consideration the children's level of maturity: it does not seem unreasonable to expect the primary school to bear this in mind and adapt accordingly.   The question is, of course, how.   The demand is for specific programmes and basic skills.   But here another question arises: should we seek general basic skills or are specific basic skills sufficient?   The latter will to an extent be determined by the type of learning programme implemented.

Despite the fact that there is always a degree of ambiguity in the issue, we feel we can safely deduce from the overall results of evaluation of the compensatory programmes both at home and abroad, that to achieve generalised basic skills is extremely difficult; this is one of the reasons why we in fact decided not to use the IQ test as our sole criterion of evaluation.

By making an analysis of the requirements to enable children to enter primary school with a hope of success, we selected a number of specific learning programmes, which were arranged in a set order, so that the child can only embark upon a given activity if he has sufficiently mastered the preceding activity.   This method is strictly adhered to, for fear of lapsing into a type of coaching which will be of no use whatsoever for the development of subsequent skills.

2.2 Procedure adopted 1976-1977

In the first year, specific exercises were tested on small groups of 4 to 8 children.   A teacher from the project team took charge of the children for an average of 3 hours weekly over a period of 6 months.   During this time the number of learning stages in the programme was examined to ensure that this was sufficient to meet pupils' needs; a pupil was only permitted to proceed to the next stage if the preceding one had been mastered.

2.2.1 Content

The learning programme consists of three main parts:
(a) Preparatory handwriting
(b) Preparatory mathematics
(c) Preparatory reading

(a) Preparatory handwriting

In addition to a number of very specific activities designed as a preparation for handwriting, there were numerous activities which served as a preparation for this and for reading.   The specific activities entailed training both gross motor skills (e.g. blackboard exercises) and fine motor skills (e.g. copying and tracing given letters such as o, e, u, m; drawing circles, squares, rectangles and triangles).

(b) Preparatory mathematics

In this field activities were limited to
- learning and using certain quantitative concepts such as more, less, much, little, as much as, long, short, small, large, equal;
- recognising the symbols used for the numbers nought to five; learning to count up to five, solving additions and subtractions (with numbers not exceeding five).

(c) Preparatory reading

For this purpose we used the following exercises:

- making analyses and syntheses of given diagrams consisting of four familiar geometric shapes: circles, triangles, squares, rectangles.
- picking out different and identical diagrams according to a given example (using drawings of both concrete objects and abstract forms, and both letters and words).
- arranging sentences.
- finding the appropriate word for a given drawing.
- learning to recognise that different letters represent different sounds.

2.2.2 Evaluation

(a) The groups

Five classes were used in the experiment. These were chosen because a pre-test showed them to contain a relatively high percentage of slow learners. Eight of the slower learners were selected from each of these classes; four were assigned at random to the experimental group and four to the control group, bringing the number of slow learners in the experimental and in the control groups to totals of twenty. For teaching as well as for research purposes twenty children were added to these groups (2 x 4 from each class) whose pre-test results indicated that they should have no difficulty in coping with primary school.

	Experimental Group	Control Group	Total
Group at risk	20	20	40
Successful learners	20	20	40
TOTAL	40	40	80

(b) Results

The special learning programme was divided into three periods. At the end of each period both the experimental group and the control group were given a series of tests.

Test 1

The first test entailed joining up pictures with lines (lines), recognising basic shapes amidst distractors (shapes), being able to identify both similar and different concrete and abstract shapes (difference/similarity), quantitative and spatial concepts. The following table reflects the extent to which the experimental group differs from the control group and the strong group from the weak group.

The experimental group clearly made proportionately more progress than the control group. There is, however, no interaction effect; both the strong group and the weak group reflect considerable progress. Broadly speaking, it can be said that the weak pupils in the experimental group reach the same level of progress as the strong pupils in the control group (53.10 in relation to 48.32).

TABLE 1

Test 1	Effect of Programme	Strong-Weak	Interaction
1. Lines	-	-	-
2. Shapes	p < .001	p < .05	-
3. Difference/Similarity	p < .001	p < .001	-
4. Quantitative & Spatial Concepts	p < .01	p < .001	-
5. TOTAL p.p.1	p < .001	p < .001	-

	Strong	Weak
Experimental	70.50	53.10
Control	48.32	32.55

Test 2

The second test consists of three parts:
- concepts - here the children's knowledge of concepts such as first, last, left, right is tested.
- distinguishing numbers amidst a series of letters.
- adding up: here the children are presented with two circles, one of which contains more dots than the other; the children have to fill in the missing dots.

TABLE 2

Test 2	Effect of Programme	Strong-Weak	Interaction
1. Concepts	p < .01	p < .05	-
2. Numbers	p < .01	p < .05	-
3. Adding up	p < .001	p < .001	p .05
4. TOTAL p.p.2	p < .001	p < .001	-

	Strong	Weak
Experimental	23.73	12.56
Control	15.73	8.31

Strong pupils profit more from the compensatory programme.

Test 3

In test three we distinguish between:
- recognising given numbers in a series of numbers and letters.
- recognising given letters in a series of other letters.
- recognising given consonants and vowels amidst other letters. We tried to teach the children to recognise these consonants and vowels by associating them both with words, with which they would be familiar (key words) and with

a matching picture, e.g. the 'f' of fire, and a picture of a fire.
- looking for matching words (word similarities).
- appropriate matching of word and picture (picture-word).

TABLE 3

Test 3	Effect of Programme	Strong-Weak	Interaction*
1. Recognising numbers	$p < .001$	$p < .001$	$p < .01$
2. Recognising letters	$p < .001$	$p < .001$	$p < .01$
3. Vowels	$p < .01$	$p < .50$	n .5
4. Consonants	$p < .001$	$p < .01$	$p < .05$
5. Word similarities	$p < .05$	$p < .05$	n .50
6. Picture-word	$p < .05$	$p < .001$	n .5
TOTAL SCORE	$p < .001$	$p < .001$	$p < .05$

*All significant interaction effects indicate that the improvement made by
the strong group is greater than that of the weak group.

	Strong	Weak
Experimental	51.63	23.00
Control	29.00	7.57

Comments

It would thus seem clearly possible to introduce specific learning programmes.
In general terms, it could be said that the weak pupils from the experimental
group achieve scores which are comparable to those of the strong pupils from the
control group. Moreover, the pupils from the strong group gave evidence of
even greater progress than the pupils from the weak group.

One might question how much effect progress in these specific learning programmes
has on the child's more general abilities. For this reason, a standard
scholastic maturity test was carried out at the end of the school year. The
results are very much what one might expect: the strong pupils achieve higher
scores than weak pupils, the experimental group achieves better results than the
control group; but only the first effect would appear to be of any significance,
in that the progress made by the experimental group was limited to more specific
items (i.e. items which bore the closest resemblance to what was specifically
taught in the programme).

Thus we see how imperative it is to analyse accurately which partial skills are
essential for the acquisition of more complex ones. We can teach children to
distinguish between different letters (obviously a prerequisite for learning to
read), but one cannot expect this to result in an improvement of the general
skill of 'visual discrimination'.

Here too we see the importance of successful learning: the different sub-stages
have to be passed so as not to run the risk of training isolated skills which
will be of no subsequent use.

2.3 <u>Procedure adopted 1977-1978</u>

Evaluation has shown that it is possible to teach most children a number of basic
skills in a minimum of time. Moreover, the children seemed positively motivated
which was probably attributable to successful learning: the set assignments,
although not easy, always remained within the range of the children's ability.
The next point was to examine whether the procedure could be carried out in an
ordinary class. Accordingly, the programme was given to the pre-school teachers,
who were asked to go through the activities with children with learning difficulties for a maximum of twenty minutes daily.

During this change-over period we encountered a number of problems. To begin
with, the majority of the teachers went through the activities just as they would
normal lessons, teaching the entire class at once. Consequently, during the
period of taking stock of progress, special emphasis was put on working in small
groups and on the differentiation of what was done according to the needs of
individual children.

As yet we have no evaluation data;   however, it does appear that the children
achieved adequate proficiency in all the activities presented.

2.3.1 <u>Contents of the programme - 'auditory skills'</u>

In addition, a number of activities pertaining to auditory skills were tested,
again on an experimental basis. These activities consist of:

- a series of exercises using worksheets
- a series of verbal activities which form the greater part of the activities.

The worksheet exercises consist of:

- looking for matching letters and short words
- recognising letters and short words which had been seen previously
- discriminating between long and short words and sentences
- indicating the number of words in a given sentence; the child must place
  as many crosses alongside a given sentence as there are words in it.

The verbal activities can be divided into two parts:

(a) activities which only involve listening;
(b) auditory analysis and synthesis.

(a) The activities involving listening can be divided into three parts:

- the ability to listen attentively to sequences of words and sentences and
  repeat them accurately
- the ability to say the first and last words after listening to sequences of
  words or a sentence
- the ability to pick out the same word in two different sequences of words or a
  sentence - e.g. The hunter shoots a <u>hare</u> and a rabbit. The <u>hare</u> can run very
  fast.

(b) Auditory analysis and synthesis entail:

- isolating and detecting auditory substructures: e.g. hook: boom - school - shook:
  in which word can we hear 'ook'?
- identifying a recurrent phoneme in pairs of words: e.g. at - tea: which letter
  (sound) can you hear twice?
- auditory synthesis of a word, separating and bringing together the initial and
  final sounds. e.g. b - all? boo - t?

- being able to rhyme using both nonsense words and actual words
- recognising a phoneme and stating its initial or final position.

2.3.2 Evaluation

At the end of the school year 1977/78, an evaluation was carried out with the two types of experimental groups. As was the case in the development of the first programme, the activities were undertaken with small groups of pupils. In each case, twenty children from two classes were picked out and randomly assigned to an experimental group and a control group, thus bringing the total number of children in the experimental group and the control group to twenty each.

In addition to this, the pre-school teacher applied the programme to her class. For this purpose a control group was formed of children from different classes, on the basis of a pre-test.

Lastly, close attention was paid to all children in the experimental group during their first year of primary school, so as to check to what extent the preparatory activities had helped them to learn to read.

2.3.3 Plans for 1978-1979

Up to this point, the special learning programme has been essentially experimental. The activities were first applied to a small group and then to the whole class. This resulted in an overall reconsideration of the nature of the activities, the number of intermediate steps, etc. Currently, an attempt is being made to integrate the activities into a more extensive programme. As a first step, the more extensive programme is being re-examined and improved where necessary.

On the whole, the pre-school activities are of a fairly general nature and the aim is to pursue several objectives. In the instance of children experiencing difficulties with any partial skills, there must be scope for intervention and further assistance. It is in this situation that the concept of integrating specific activities becomes meaningful. After a period of three months an overall test is carried out: children who exhibit learning difficulties (retard-ation) in any particular sector are accordingly coached, by using the specific activity programme. Retardation, in this case, has a fairly specific meaning. Activities geared towards meeting the requirements of reading, writing and arith-metic are spaced out over an entire year in view of the experimental development of the programme. These activities were integrated into the more extensive programme.

Specific coaching is only given to children who have not achieved set objectives. It is possible that the retardation of some might still remain. This will be immediately apparent in that these children will be unable to master partial skills, in which case it would be necessary to back-track to activities geared towards a lower level of development. An attempt has already been made with a group of nine of these children, to find out just how far back one has to go; the gap appears to have been bridged by six children to date. A more systematic involvement of the younger age groups (three to four year olds) in this project will enable us to deal with these problems more thoroughly.

Conclusions of the Ghent Enrichment and Stimulation Project

1. Starting Points

1.1 General

The failure rate right at the start of primary schooling is striking, particularly in the case of those children from economically, socially and culturally weak environments. It seems that the environment at least partially accounts for this failure rate. The effects of environmental handicaps are not totally irreversible.

The problem is not always purely an intellectual problem either. General personality traits, the nature of social relationships, the level and nature of motivation, self-image and the extent to which one feels accepted and secure, can equally influence school failure.

Nor is it only a question of retardation, but also of a type of experience, of a sub-culture, which differ from that of the middle class. The experience and culture of children from the lower social levels are not sufficiently valued in contemporary society and in the school, in which they may function poorly. From an educational point of view, this means that education and the stimulation necessary for development are in part functions of the experiences provided by the environment, by the child's sub-culture. This sub-culture must be made as functional as possible in terms of schooling, without obliging a child to remain on a lower level or obstructing change. The difficulty lies in achieving a balance between recognising and valuing the sub-culture on the one hand, and the stimulation of improvement and change on the other. Where is the boundary between respect for the culture and giving it its proper value, on the one hand, and stimulating and thus modifying it on the other? How can the two be combined? The task is all the more difficult in view of the fact that, differentiation apart, movement towards a general cultural pattern is probably essential.

Mental retardation, too - in the strictest sense of the word - is a possible consequence of an insufficiently stimulating environment. Although one must guard against the premature interpretation of being 'different' as necessarily being 'inferior', it is not enough to interpret 'inferior' development simply as being 'different'. A stimulating education, including relationships within a generally sound culture, is useful, along with respect for the values of the original sub-culture of the child.

Little is known about the <u>psychological characteristics</u> of children from socially, economically and culturally 'weak' environments, and because of this they are all the more difficult to ascertain objectively.   The complex attributes involved may vary according to individual reactions.   The consequences of any deficiency may differ greatly according to the total context in which it occurs.

1.2 <u>Phases in the screening of environmental influences</u>

Socio-cultural handicap is significant long before starting school.   Direct experience in a stimulating environment is of the utmost importance from the first year of life.   Therefore educational action exerted upon the families is desirable.   The influence of the crèche too, is very clear.   This varies enormously, according to its quality.   Systematic stimulation in an effectively protective climate is essential in this case too.   Day nurseries and pre-kinder-gartens may also provide a stimulating or a strongly 'handicapping' influence.

The following sections focus chiefly on children of 5 to 7 years of age.

1.3 <u>Transition from pre-school to primary school</u>

Without disregarding the importance of inherited, constitutional differences, it can be said that the realisation of the child's potential is to a large extent dependent upon the experience and the stimulation provided by the environment. Hence the great importance of the child's early years, the influence of which is difficult to define.   On the pre-school level, however, supplementary deficien-cies and handicaps can be avoided; and we must not overlook the fact that there is still scope for stimulation, protection and adaptation - provided suitable means are employed.

Although few children achieve the fullest possible development in their environ-ment, it would appear that in our population the group which is clearly socially handicapped constitutes a minority.   The non-optimal development of the majority - or of everyone - is less obvious, but just as real.

The interest in the child and in his education would appear to be of considerable importance to his development, along with other positive stimuli.   This is true in the case of the family, but also of the institutional educational environment. Broadly speaking, next to the education provided by the home, the parents' atti-tude towards the school seems to be an important variable.   This implies the need to involve the parents in the school.   An obvious step in the first stage is an intensive form of home-school social work.

2. <u>Strategies</u>

2.1 <u>General</u>

Treating the <u>causes</u> of the deficiencies and the difficulties is by far preferable to a treatment of the <u>symptoms</u> only.   On the other hand, some symptoms, i.e. the consequences of inhibiting environmental situations, may have an obstructing effect on subsequent developmental processes and thus give rise to increased retardation.   Consequently, the treatment of symptoms cannot be totally excluded.

Compensation, as it was developed abroad in compensatory programmes, can be useful - by removing direct deficiencies related to experience and linguistic ability, for instance.   This is important mainly because it would appear that these skills have a multiplier effect.These programmes, however, centred strongly on motor skills and intellectual ability; their purpose was to prepare the child, in a superficial and prescriptive manner, for academic learning.

For socially handicapped children, this may lessen initial educational difficulties.   In our situation, the children concerned almost invariably require continuous help.   However, stimulation from an early stage in the child's life is
essential, and continues to be extremely useful afterwards, particularly when it
is applied broadly.

More general stimulation is necessary if it is to have any real effect.   A
variety of possible applications - not necessarily mutually exclusive - can be
distinguished.

A first possibility is in an action for general social and educational reform.
This implies fundamental choices in relation to objectives which have still to be
attained and to strategies which have still to be applied.   However, this
undoubtedly important issue lies outside our remit.   We could only consider
exerting direct influence on the development of the children via either the
family or the school.

2.1.1 Social action with particular reference to influence on the family

Social action must pay particular attention to the forms of control used by
parents, and to the nature of their educational attitude.   The early educational
environment (and ensuring its continuity) is important here.   Except in
particular circumstances, influencing the family environment would nevertheless
appear to be a difficult, delicate procedure, involving an enormous amount of
intensive work.

2.1.2 School strategies (including psychological techniques for intervention)

Notwithstanding the considerable importance of the earliest period of childhood
and the family environment in general, both the crèche and the school environment
would appear equally to be obvious areas for modification and stimulation strategies.   Although the influence of the school is less fundamental than that of
the family, the school is nonetheless the ideal environment for intervention.
It is, in any event, possible to ensure that learning in school (in a broad as
well as a narrow sense) is more successful than has been the case up till now.
This is true for the pre-kindergarten, the pre-school, primary school, secondary
education and beyond.

The following form the basis of the school strategies:

(i) Valuing of the home environment of the child, its experience and its
accomplishments - without allowing this to result in a lack of stimulation, or in
difficulties of integrating well with the group belonging to the dominant culture.
This is the basis of all the following proposals.

(ii) Protection, a positive affective climate, positive social relations with
adults and peers, a feeling of acceptance, a positive self-image, creative
stimulation, exploration - all of these, without becoming over-protective, without
neglecting to help the children to cope with frustration and to assimilate rules
which protect them from aggression.

(iii) Opportunities for exploration and self-realisation (with respect and
understanding for others), for stimulating experience (including social experience)
discoveries and thought-provoking activity.

2.2 Some aspects of a stimulation strategy

(i) General, broad stimulation of experience, of forms of arrangement and
assimilation, both on a broad personality plane as in the field of thought and

the execution of tasks, with particular attention to security, self-image, independence, creativity, motivation and social relations.

All this demands the establishment of a systematic, structured, all-encompassing strategy with specific inbuilt strategies. The development of the strategy must, however, be characterised by spontaneity and freedom, and because this extends the work beyond the particularly intellectual aspects, more specific techniques are necessary.

(ii) Ensuring the successful learning of each stage in the programme too, helps to raise the average level without depriving more scholastically able children of stimuli necessary for their development.

(iii) The intervention offered by specific programmes and group activities for scholastically less able children is only meaningful when it is the backcloth to the broader educational context which caters for it.   Here the following points are important:

a) Awareness of objectives, i.e. awareness of the more general long-term objectives in addition to those which must be achieved immediately.

b) Sensitivity to problems and opportunities for stimulation, which presupposes knowledge of the full range of possibilities as well as an awareness of those already in use.

c) Group work

d) Close cooperation and interaction between the school authorities, the educational advisers and the teachers. Without those, there is no hope of realising the general aims of the head, the practical goals still to be achieved, or even the proposed overall strategy.

(iv) Differentiation - by using an approach such as learning in stages, supplemented by group work, less able children can be greatly helped. For the time being, the differences between individuals and between groups cannot be expected to diminish. Improved teaching methods will perceptibly raise the average, but will not remove the differences. There is, after all, a strong possibility that those children who are more gifted and least handicapped socially will respond most quickly to general educational stimulation, and this susceptibility must certainly not be thwarted. Compensation must ensure that additional help is given to the handicapped children without this happening.

It must be stressed once again that the obligatorily structured nature of the stimulation strategy must under no circumstances result only in cognitive learning, nor must it restrict either spontaneity or creativity, both of which should be a first requirement of the programme.

3. Conclusions Concerning Educational Innovation

3.1 Approaches

(i) Providing the appropriate educational climate.

(ii) Defining working objectives.

(iii) Establishing strategies which support an active learning approach.

(iv) Constant evaluation on all levels and in various contexts:

a) Despite the difficulty of evaluating the effectiveness of the above strategies, it must still be attempted. Evaluation of special strategies must occur within the context of general stimulation (this applies to the control group as much as to the experimental group) in order to gauge the specific effect of the specific strategies. From a technical standpoint, this type of evaluation is relatively simple.

b) For a summative evaluation, more attention has to be given to the development of appropriate instruments which are <u>valid</u> and <u>reliable</u>. In the past, IQ tests were too frequently used in the summative evaluation of stimulation schemes, and these can give an inaccurate picture particularly in the case of ineffectual programmes. A good IQ test in particular may be completely inappropriate for the evaluation of the results of stimulation.

c) Laboratory tests to evaluate learning situations are often in their style and content too dissimilar to the tasks and contexts of the classroom. Investigation precisely adapted to the real situations in class is greatly needed. Formative evaluation can provide a starting point for this.

The motivation and the child-centredness in the teacher are essential. Concerted action concerning points (i), (ii), (iii) and (iv) above, coupled with a knowledge of the child, can sensitise teachers to problems and possible interventions. All of these are necessary to provide the foundations upon which the whole activities programme is built.

3.2 Institutions

(i) Clearly defined but flexible aims of the authorities responsible for the school, and a genuine interest in the above points.

(ii) Interaction between the authorities, including the head, and teachers.

(iii) In addition, educational innovation demands intensive but flexible guidance which will quickly stimulate personal initiative. Educational innovation is impossible without the provision of adequate guidance. Its absence not only increases the insecurity of the teachers, but lowers results as an immediate consequence. It is necessary to provide written examples of activities and to back up with workshop training sessions, in addition to general information, demonstration and sustained evaluation. The teachers must come to accept the evaluation and not to feel threatened in any way by it. Indeed, it is essential that the teacher be involved continuously and actively in the innovation and in its ongoing evaluation.

Only in this manner can essential educational reform result.

3.3 Structure

(i) In general the transition from pre-school to primary school would appear to present difficulties for approximately a quarter of all children. There is a need to work towards integration of the pre-school and primary school. The transition should be smooth, and take into account the individual potential of every child.

(ii) Systematic, creative and flexible stimulation, and possibly compensatory action, is essential from the earliest stage in the child's education as well as in the transition to primary school. These must continue to be promoted in primary school in an atmosphere which, particularly in the first year of learning, must correspond to the spontaneous and protective atmosphere of the pre-school on the one hand, and to the increasing all round maturity of the child on the other. The satisfactory prolongation of active learning situations from the pre-school into the primary school would, on the basis of our experience, seem desirable.

Tactics for teaching the 3 R's should be prepared and applied at the appropriate time, without being allowed to polarise the entire programme, and above all, prescriptive formalism must be avoided.

There is every reason to give increased attention to stimulation strategies, not only in the pre-schools, but also in the crèches, the pre-kindergartens and the nurseries, in a general educational climate of protection, stimulation and spontaneity.

3.4 Training the teachers

Teacher training should match the proposed educational innovation and should emphasise child-centredness.   Next to educational guidance this is essential for success.

Basic training must have a point of reference which is derived from firsthand practical experience.   In addition, attention should be given to making the teachers aware of all sorts of problems and experiences, including those related to the situation of the socially handicapped child.   Training in personal contact should precede didactic training, because it is this that determines all educational possibilities.   The teacher must be well adjusted emotionally and highly motivated.

Much still remains to be achieved in the training of teachers for crèches, day nurseries and pre-kindergartens.

3.5 Scientific research

In general, we feel that educational innovation pays too little attention to scientific research.

(i)   Evaluative research is essential in educational innovation.   Experience shows that individual bias is extremely difficult to avoid: extensive evaluative research in this whole area would be worthwhile and instructive in itself.   This raises a number of problems, both with regard to the research design and the instruments used (evaluation criteria).

(ii) Scientific research into the determinants of the classroom situation is urgently needed.   We should like to advocate direct observation of the classroom situation itself.   Laboratory-type artificial situations (mainly teaching tests) give rise to serious problems of generalisation; on the other hand, research in real classroom situations may be so complex as to force us to neglect important aspects of day-to-day situations.

Part 3

Socio-cultural Differences and the Improvement of Education in School: 2 to 7 Year Old Children

Summary and conclusions of the research undertaken by the Department of Educational Research of the University of Liège

Prof. G. de Landsheere

M. Detheux-Jehin

E. Leclercq-Boxus

G. Manni

J. Paquay-Beckers

A. M. Thirion

M. L. Willems-Carels

In collaboration with

M. T. Wannyn-Loret

R. de Bal

Introduction: Basic Options

Most compensatory education programmes are based upon a negative view of particular social environments. An increasing number of investigations demonstrate the role not only of individual and family characteristics, but also that of the school itself as causes of academic failure.

> "Selection based on level of basic achievement is both unfair to children
> and costly to governments, because it leads to segregation within the
> school and to the growth of remedial education outside the school. The
> less effectively the school plays its part, the greater the need for
> remedial education." (1)

Without taking a one-sided view of such findings, research on the effects of socio-cultural differences calls for an examination of the conditions necessary to the true democratisation of education. That is why our team held to certain major choices, throughout the changes in concepts, methods of intervention and increasing insights that arose in the course of our work.

Action in the school

Our efforts have throughout been focused on the school, not only because that was where our professional strengths lay, but because of the Belgian situation. Eighty-five per cent of children over three years old attend pre-school. Children from the most deprived socio-economic conditions are the first to begin pre-school, and stay there the longest. Despite this extension of pre-primary school, however, the failure rate at the start of compulsory education remains high, and is linked to social background.

Abandonment of the symptomatic approach

The findings of the first two years of the project led us to go beyond a diagnostic approach and to adopt a more dynamic attitude to development and the differences observed. Functional analysis in particular has been preferred for the study of a child's interactions with its school environment and to integrate formative evaluation in the intervention programmes. The objectives that all children should achieve have been centred on developmental criteria in the pre-school and on fundamental acquisitions in the primary school.

Research and action

Research cannot be distinct from the daily work of the school if it is to stand the test of reality.   Hence, all partners in the educational enterprise (mainly the teachers so far as we are concerned) must be involved.

The concept of 'compensatory education' was slowly replaced by that of 'mastery learning', the aim of which is to enhance development and learning in the school environment.   The aim is to guarantee to all children the right and the means of acquiring the basic skills and thus move from an élitist, selective pedagogy to a more all-embracing one.

A greater variety of methods of intervention has been devised to match this greater unity in the formulation of the problem.   In addition to classical experimental tests and design, we have added descriptive and interpretative methods to take account of the complexity and novelty of action research and of its relation to the general socio-political background.

REFERENCE

(1) Report of a work group, in Compensatory Education. Council of Europe, Strasbourg, 1975, p.79.

1 Development of the Research

1. First Phase (1969-1971)

The first phase of the research was characterised by differential studies which aimed to specify the psychological characteristics of working-class children.

Studies related to:

(i)   Sociological description of all children attending pre-school in the town of Liège (1).

(ii) The development of praxes and gnoses of the language (2).

(iii) Cognitive processes (3).

(iv) The prediction of school attainment (4).

These studies have shown not only the connection between the different aspects of development and socio-economic background, but also the effect of different educational environments on standards of work. For instance, characteristics such as content, ways of test administration and the number of pictures in the verbal tests produced differences in syntactical constructions which were independent of the children's social origin.

Generally speaking, these studies gave rise to a re-examination of the concepts and methods of comparative studies (5) to which we shall return when we deal with cognitive development (see section headed 'infant school').

From the beginning of the research, an extensive project was conducted in a school chosen in accordance with social criteria. A study of the records of the Fund for Financial Assistance to Families with Children attending School, and of the geographical distribution of help to the most needy families in Liège, identified a school situated in an area where concentrated financial aid was being given to a predominantly Belgian population. Our work was thus carried out in a school in a working-class district in cooperation with the teachers, without undertaking any special educational activity outside the class, and without setting up any new teacher category which would have needed extra staff.

To get away from the concept of school failure and its consequential emphasis on remedial education to compensate deficits, we started from the theory of Piaget and from one of its specific applications, namely, C. Kamii's (6) programme which

seems to escape the criticisms levelled at most compensatory programmes. Apart
from the soundness of its conceptual framework, this programme had the advantage
of fitting well with Belgian pre-school traditions and of providing solutions for
the definition of objectives, the choice of educational situations and the
establishment of formative rather than normative evaluation.

1.1   Procedure

Organising the interplay between theory and practice

Seminars bringing together teachers and researchers were organised to ensure the
interplay between the conceptualization of objectives and theoretical knowledge
on the one hand, and day-to-day experience on the other. What did we wish to
do? when? how? and, more particularly, why?

Encouragement of cooperative activity in the classroom

The aim of having the researchers present regularly in the classes was to make
concrete and adjust to each age group, the objectives defined by the seminars.
It became gradually clear that the structure of the class itself would have to
change to ensure individualisation of learning and to try out methods adapted to
each child's level of development.

Participating in socio-cultural activities

Work in the classroom showed once again that the pursuit of objectives such as
autonomy and freedom of expression, demands a fundamental change in relationships
and in the educational environment. Moreover, the discontinuity between different aspects of school life became strikingly apparent: crèche, class periods,
meals and socio-cultural activities seemed to constitute independent entities.
We decided to deal with the children directly in all these activities, and to
become, in their eyes, "different" adults.

1.2   Results and comments

During this first phase the main measurable change was in the results of tests of
operations and in verbal tests. The experimental group scored higher than the
controls. The progress made by the children from a deprived environment was
higher than or equal to that of children in general; the reverse was the case
for the controls. These positive effects are not to be despised, even if they
do merely reflect progress in terms of the educational programme.

What was the effect of the seminars? It seems likely that they led to a richer
and more adequate utilisation of the educational material by the teachers. The
change is noticeable not only in what they do, but in their attitudes - certain
children formerly ignored actually began to exist as individuals in the eyes of
their teachers.

However, the seminars, rather than, as we had hoped, resulting in a genuine
mutual interpretation of theory and practice, in fact confronted the teachers
with an educational model chosen by scientists, which was at once close to their
own (whence a subtle form of resistance to change: 'We always did things that way')
and seen as too demanding (giving rise to complaints and justifications: 'We
would never be able to do things that way'). We probably created a 'shopwindow
effect'(7) which often accompanies the usual ways of passing on knowledge.

The main problem facing the researcher was 'finding his place'. Confronted with
the deficiencies observed we were tempted to supply all the skills that were
lacking: psychologists, nurses, social workers, leaders. By taking part in
socio-cultural activities, we fully explored every possibility inherent in the

compensatory role. We met, but did not solve, the problem peculiar to 'alternative' schools, that of an effective relationship between child and adult, a rapport which calls for a constant re-examination of educational practices, and in the last resort implies a critical analysis of the school. This experiment also convinced us that the researcher alone cannot be the direct agent of change.

2. Second Phase (1972-1975)

In the course of the third year, efforts were centred on three problems considered crucial in the light of our sociological investigation and the results of the first period.

The sociological investigation showed that the pre-kindergartens, which are small classes annexed to pre-schools to cater for the one-and-a-half to three-year olds, are mainly attended by working-class children. Direct ethologically inspired observation enabled us to describe the interactions of young children with the educational environment. The research and the project in the pre-kindergarten led the researchers to ask about the social factors, to examine institutions for young children, particularly the crèches, and to raise questions about the employment of women in Belgium.

The methodology of cooperation in curriculum development for the pre-school was examined in depth.

Continuous observation of the population finishing the first primary school year showed that results from the tests used (tests of operations, verbal tests, tests of reading and mathematical attainment) were lower in the experimental group. It seemed thus, that although the pre-school may be a propitious time for intervention, such intervention must be continued throughout the compulsory schooling period. With this in mind, the instruments and methods of mastery learning were developed for the basic skills and applied to the first year primary school classes.

The table shows the development of the research and the projects which were carried out simultaneously in the pre-kindergartens, in the pre-school and at the start of compulsory schooling. It also shows the continuity and spread which were possible - the development of strategies of formative evaluation related to the initial and continuing training of pre-school and primary teachers, an examination of the institutions themselves, and activity in the education of children from 0 - 3 in collaboration with women's voluntary organisations.

DEVELOPMENT OF THE RESEARCH (second phase)

	EARLY CHILDHOOD	PRE-SCHOOL	FIRST YEAR
1971–1972	Psychological observation and intervention in the pre-kindergarten of the pilot school	Cooperative development of a curriculum inspired by Piaget	Development of instruments and methods for mastery learning in reading and mathematics
1972–1973	Extension of the observation to the 13 pre-kindergartens in the city of Liège; Differential study of cognitive development		Application of the mastery-learning technique to reading and mathematics in some first year primary school classes
1973–1974	Questionnaire given to all teachers and nursery nurses in the pre-kindergartens; Organisation of seminars with the pre-kindergarten teachers and nursery nurses	Participation in seminars on in-service training for pre-school teachers; Development of educative activities with a group of pre-school teachers	Prediction of learning with regard to reading & mathematics; Introduction of the PREDIC method in collaboration with the child guidance centres + the primary inspectorate
1974–1975	Extension of the observation to all the crèches in the city of Liège; Sociological study of working women in Belgium	Development of a training scheme involving micro-teaching in pre-school teacher training colleges	Formative & continuous evaluation of learning with regard to reading; Seminar on initial & in-service training in State teacher training colleges
1975–1976	Sociological study of the schooling of women in Belgium; Participation in the action undertaken by women's voluntary movements		Experimental development & validation of mastery-learning strategies in relation to mathematics with groups of teachers

NOTES AND REFERENCES

(1) Pichault, M. Les enfants des écoles maternelles de la ville de Liège et leur milieu social. Université de Liège. Laboratoire de Pédagogie expérimentale et Institut de Sociologie. (1972)

(2) Detheux-Jehin, M., Manni G. (1973) Etude différentielle du développement psycholinguistique, in Recherche en Education. 1. Direction Generale de l'Organisation des Etudes, Bruxelles, 1973.

(3) Paquay-Beckers, J., Thirion, A.M. Etude différentielle du développement cognitif, ibidem.

(4) LeClerq-Boxus, E. Etude différentielle de la prédiction du rendement en lecture en première année primaire. ibidem.

(5) Etude des caractéristiques psychologiques et sociologiques des enfant défavorises par leur milieu. Bulletin d'Information, Conseil de l'Europe,1. 1974.

(6) Kamii, C. (1971) Evaluation of Learning in Preschool Education, in B.S.Bloom, J.T.Hastings, C.Madaus (eds) Handbook of Formative and Summative Evaluation of Student Learning, McGraw-Hill, New York.

(7) "Popularisation 'shows' us knowledge; it makes us see its factors and its products but at the same time convinces us that we will never be rich enough to make these our own. It places the scientists themselves behind the shop window, in another and inaccessible context." Translation from: Roqueplo, P., Le Partage du Savoir, Sciences, Culture, Popularisation, Seuil, Paris, 1974, p.166.

2 The Two-year-old Child in Groups: Direct Observation, Action and the Study of Institutions

In 1972 we drew attention to the necessity of a study of the pre-kindergarten classes (1) at the local level – the child's first contact with the school at a critical point in development, the fact that the majority of such children came from a socio-economically deprived environment (2).

The work conducted from September 1971 until September 1974 comprised:

- Observation of the behaviour of children in the pre-kindergarten
- Educational action in collaboration with the teachers, and institutional analysis
- A study of the infant reception centres in Belgium.

These three categories can be distinguished by the methods used and by specific content: they complement one another in the study. Observations of children carried out in different pre-kindergartens in the City of Liège spotlighted the real situations facing teachers and caused us to move from the strictly educational 'how' to the institutional 'how' and to the 'why' (organisation of care for children aged 0 to 3 years in Belgium, the working status of women).

1. Observation

1.1 Objectives

To describe the behaviour of children, child-child and adult-child relationships, and relations with objects, as they are seen in the pre-kindergarten classes in the City of Liège. This account of the children's behaviour has to be related to variables describing the child (age, length of time at school, sex, socio-cultural origins) and with factors in the institution itself (influence of the care givers and of opportunities offered to the child).

The work had two phases: the development of observational techniques in one class (3) and then generalisation in all the classes of the town of Liège.

1.2 Methods

Direct observation of a sample of children and of those who come into contact with them. All behaviour was recorded on the tape and then categorised into imitation, gesture, movements, with a specification of the subject and object of the behaviour.

111

Various analyses were made:

- Classification of behaviour according to the movement and part of the body involved.
- Classification of object manipulation according to a developmental hierarchy.
- Judgements of certain relationships between children: attack, attention-seeking, placatory, non-violent responses to aggression.
- Classification of adult behaviour according to its function (care, control, educational action, positive contact, neutral action, group regulation) (4).

1.3 Sample and experimental design (Observational study)

Sample: 195 children, fifteen children from each of the thirteen pre-kindergarten classes in the city of Liège (i.e. almost all the children attending this type of school).

The research design had the following practical constraints:

- Three observers.
- Each observer spent a day in each of the thirteen classes, the observations were thus spread over three weeks (13 school days).
- In each class, observation was made of five activities: free play, board games, group activities, washing one's hands, crèche. A different child was observed for each individual activity. Each observation unit (i.e. a child involved in one activity) lasted five minutes.

The sample was not stratified on the basis of the independent variables. The population observed corresponds exactly to the total pre-kindergarten population; as many girls as boys, few children from privileged socio-economic environments.

1.4 Results

The direct observation made in the pre-kindergarten permits a description of the behaviour of children aged 2 to 3 in group contexts without interpreting the explicit content of this behaviour or its underlying intention or emotions. This motor behaviour was related to that of the adult whose task it is to look after the children.

From the analysis of these observations the following picture emerges:

The pre-kindergarten child spends as much time watching other children and adults as it does in manipulating objects. The child's watching behaviour is thus of considerable importance.

From a more general viewpoint, social relationships make up one third of the observed behaviour. Relations with others consist primarily (quantitatively) of exchanges with peers. Gestural provocations and verbalized inviting or placatory behaviour between children are about equally frequent.

As for the relationships with adults, these are similar whether in the class with the preschool teacher, or in the crèche with the nursery nurse; the children watch the teacher or nursery nurse a great deal (75 per cent of their behaviour towards her) and speak less to her than to their peers.

And how do the adults, observed incidentally during the study of the children, behave?

The preschool teacher divides her attention between the group as a whole and the children taken individually. In front of the class, she is concerned primarily with educational procedures (74 per cent on average of her behaviour). On the other hand, when dealing individually with the children under observation, she intervenes to control conduct (40 per cent of her behaviour) and to look after physical needs.

In the crèche where there are fewer children, the nursery nurse establishes a more individual contact with the children, but this is just as much for purposes of control as it is in the case of the preschool teacher.

Apart from social relationships, one third of the children's behaviour is directed towards objects (the remaining third includes the child's conduct towards itself as well as towards non-identifiable objects). If we consider the group of objects most frequently used (board games, small toys like dolls, large toys, classroom materials), the board games take precedence. If the objects are considered individually, it is the classroom furniture which is most often used. Next in order come cubes and lego blocks, dolls and cars, objects which promote large motor activity, particularly vehicles (bicycles, tractors).

It is surprising how little use is made of certain material (such as water, sand, earth), certain toys (balls, household utensils, musical instruments, toboggans, rocking horses, the shop, puppets), certain accessories (mirrors, floor covering), at a period of the child's life during which psychologists talk of intense and widespread motor experimentation, of exploration of the world, of symbolic play and of language development.

Observation of how objects are handled reveals that the activities which predominate are those which the child establishes early on in development: grasping, touching, pushing, throwing, rubbing (65 per cent of behaviour towards objects). Far less frequent are activities concerning spatial organisation, balancing and exploring activities. 'Games of make believe', with or without an object which, some psychologists claim, appear as characteristic behaviour between 21 and 24 months, constitute only a very small part of the behaviour observed in 2 to 3 year old children in these particular situations.

Clearly, this descriptive account of the pre-kindergarten is not complete. The results must be looked at more closely in the light of certain other variables.

When one considers the variables related to the child (sex, age, socio-economic level) it can be seen at once that even in the context of motor behaviour, which has not been closely examined, there is no such thing as a typical 2 to 3-year old child, but rather little boys and girls, children who are either 'deprived' or 'privileged'. The pre-kindergarten establishment, because of the educational aims of those who run it, does not have the same meaning for all children.

Variables linked with the type of organisation of the pre-kindergarten must also be taken into account. Is the nursery situation different from that of nursery school classroom? If so, with what is this difference connected? staff training (nursery nurses and pre-school teachers), the number of children, of which there are many more in the class than in the nursery?

Moreover, in order to interpret the significance of the pre-kindergarten data, the same type of observation should be undertaken of the 2 to 3-year old child in its family environment and elsewhere.

In the course of the year 1974-1975, undergraduate students in Educational Sciences from the University of Liège conducted an observation, similar to the one we did in the pre-kindergarten classes, in the crèches in the city of Liège. The observation was carried out on eighty children, i.e. sixteen children in each of the five sections for older children in three crèches in the city of Liège (three of the four existing crèches).

The research design was devised to allow sixteen students to make observations. Each student spent one entire day in each of the five sections. There five children were observed in five activities (free morning play, free afternoon play, large group activities, small group activities, tidying up). Four hundred observation units were thus obtained.

The data are currently being analysed. The results of this observation will make it possible to interpret those of the pre-kindergarten more satisfactorily. Moreover, we shall have a body of observations which, despite its limitations, will make discussion realistic and still be based on a group, on an institution, rather than simply on a normative individual description of a child.

2. Study of Institutions

Observation conducted in the field allows the research workers to witness the life of the class.

A questionnaire sent to thirteen preschool teachers and thirteen nursery nurses in the pre-kindergarten made it possible to be more specific about topics which had arisen in the course of conversation: the problems posed by a class of young children, the current and ideal organisation of the pre-kindergarten, the pre-kindergarten as a social institution.

At meetings, the teachers raised the 'hows' connected with the school: how does the pre-kindergarten fit into the general school system and into society as a whole?; what is the nature of the relationship between the teachers and the authorities, and with those who make use of it, the parents? Unwittingly, pre-school teachers and nursery nurses raised the question 'why?': why do we have pre-kindergartens?, why do we have creches? These questions led the discussion to the social level: what are problems raised by the employment of women, what social functions do different institutions, and particularly the educational ones, fulfil?

We have also been led to consider early child care in Belgium.

3. Centres receiving young children

The diversity of sources to which one has to refer in order to compile a list of arrangements for caring for young children reveals how complex the problem of child care is in Belgium. It is shared between the Ministry of Public Health, State Education and the private sector, the latter being subject to a more or less strict supervision depending on the situation and, in most cases, being fee paying.

Moreover, the problem of child care is always linked with another problem: that of the working woman. We note at once that the size of the female working population is not related to the number of public institutions nor to the number of children within them. In Belgium, the great disparity between the percentages of the relevant age group who attend crèches (14 per cent of children under three) and preschool (95 per cent of the children over three) illustrates the different status and function of these institutions. This state of affairs is not without effect on the parents' attitude towards the institution, and on the attitude of staff in charge of the children towards the parents.

Sociologists have shown that differences in the social composition of the groups of children attending nursery schools have repercussions on the objectives of the institutions (5). In bringing together children from all social environments, the preschool today is adjusting to changes in the social definition of early childhood. We are no longer content with physical and emotional care; what might be called cultural care is also demanded. This cultural care takes its place in the school curriculum and becomes the subject of specific educational action (6). For this reason one might expect that more crèches attended by children from all social backgrounds would extend their educational role. But we doubt whether mass school attendance is by itself the unique condition bringing about change for the benefit of working class children. At least this is what the conditions in preschools today seem to suggest.

A survey of preschool populations in the city of Liège establishes the link between inferior socio-cultural environment, attendance at pre-kindergartens, very early entry into preschool (all the social classes are represented around the age of 3) and, above all, attendance at the school canteens and the crèches (7). Children below two-and-a-half years old (30 months) who are unable to attend pre-kindergartens, which are too few in number, find their way into the nursery schools. Hence, those who require the greatest attention are admitted into the least favourable environment for them. It can thus be affirmed that: 'the segregation, against which the school is fighting, has begun to take effect before the school is legally able to admit children'. (8)

These findings clearly show that 'the combination of the requirements for care and education, which varies according to social status, can lead to the preschool being used in different ways, despite the apparent similarity of prevalence of school attendance and of age of entry'. (7)

Indeed, we are all aware of the limitations of the school in our society even though it is open to all and is free. It reproduces the social class structure, and the traditional male-female roles; it excludes political and social realities; it favours individualism and competition. It remains a closed world, the realm of the specialist. (9)

4. Further Developments

Communications between research workers and educators came about as a result of the observations carried out in the field.

It was the questions posed by educators which obliged the research workers to consider the institutions and to take account of the organisation of reception centres for the under-threes, the working status of women and the political potential they represent.

This institutional reflection made possible the starting of an action research in collaboration with two Belgian women's voluntary movements: 'Progressive Women Socialists' and 'Women's Life' (a Christian movement). These two popular education movements which are directed at those who make use of the reception facilities for young children, could very well constitute important grass-roots pressure groups (in the crèches, schools). They similarly represent a possibility for action at the governmental and parliamentary level. In movements of this kind, the foremost problems presented are of an institutional order (school expenditure, the regulations and status of the institution, the training and position of the educator), and it is against this background that questions concerned with the running of the school, the activities to be undertaken with children, and problems of the development of children emerge. In this context research workers are not only obliged to 'socialize' their knowledge but to put a different order of psychological and educational questions.

NOTES AND REFERENCES

(1) Classes annexed to certain nursery schools in the City of Liège which are attended by 2 to 3-year old children. Unlike all other solutions to the problem of early childhood reception centres (crèches, pre-kindergartens, private kindergartens) the pre-kindergarten classes are free and depend administratively upon the local education authority (L'Echevinat de l'Instruction Publique).

(2) Manni, G. et Willems-Carels, M.L. L'aceuil des enfants de 2 à 3 ans, in Recherche en Education. Direction Générale de l'Organisation des Etudes, Bruxelles, 1973.

(3) See Manni, G. et Willems-Carels, M.L. op.cit.

(4) For the method, see De Landsheere, G., Introduction à la Recherche en Education, A. Colin-Bourrelier, Paris (1976), pp.62-67.

(5) Plaisance, E., Baudelot, O. L'évolution des objectifs de l'école maternelle, C.R.E.S.A.S., Paris, cahier No.9, 1973.

(6) Chamboredon, J.C., Prevot, J. Le 'metier d'enfant', définition sociale de la prime enfance et fonctions differentielles de l'école maternelle. R. Franc. sociol., 14, 295-335 (1973)

(7) Pichault, M. Les enfants des écoles maternelles de la ville de Liège et leur milieu social. Université de Liège, Laboratoire de Pédagogie experimentale et Institut de Sociologie. (1972)

(8) Jaumain, J. Rénovation de l'éducation prescolaire. Revue de la Direction de l'Organisation des Etudes, 9th year, No.2, February 1974.

(9) For a full discussion of the problem, see Les cahiers du Grif: Les femmes et les enfants d'abord, No.9-10, Bruxelles, December 1975; and in particular, Carels, M.L. et Manni, G., De l'enfant désire à la crèche de nos désirs.

3 Cooperative Development of a Curriculum for the Nursery School

Intervention at the nursery school level had the same theoretical basis as that of the first phase of intervention. Differential studies were conducted parallel to the action research. The aim of the Piagetian tasks of concrete operational thinking is to describe the cognitive processes of the children in positive terms, to understand the structurisation process and to determine which action is most satisfactory for the development of those operational structures which are both indispensable and common to all.

1. Differential Study of Cognitive Development: Results and Comments

1.1 Samples and tests

The Piagetian tasks were carried out on representative samples, and orthogonalized in relation to three variables: age (5-6 years old), sex and socio-economic background (three categories based on a combination of occupational and educational levels of the parents).

The first sample of 120 children was tested on six tasks: seriation, construction and language, opposites, ordination, conservation of number and conservation of substance.

In a second sample made up of 86 children, the cognitive development tests were supplemented by a test of the relation between wholes and component parts and two well known tests: the Progressive Matrices of Raven and the sub-tests of eye-motor coordination, of figure-ground discrimination, spatial relations and position in space from the Frostig Perceptual Development test.

1.2 The results

The correlations among the criterion variables are highly significant and make it possible to suggest the presence of a veritable complex based on the test of topological order (and Frostig's test) in direct relation to number and seriation. This structure, which is characterised by spatial relations linked with qualitative logic, could be the sign of the much earlier development of schemas of an infra-logical kind.

Tests selected because they were thought to be formally equivalent in what they measured, reveal relative discrepancies and/or similarities because aspects of what they purported to measure were not developing simultaneously.

Multiple regression analyses show that the environment is still the best predictor of performance on the criterion tests.   The influence of the environment is particularly noticeable in those non-verbal tests which demand the construction of spatial relations, i.e. those which constitute a privileged sub-group within the structure of criterion variables and which would have been attained at an earlier stage.   Age improves prediction except in the case of topological order and relations between wholes and parts.   The sex variable has no influence whatsoever.

The results of children from both deprived and average environments reveal an identical pattern, the differences being essentially quantitative.   The order of difficulty of items, however, is different for children from privileged back-grounds and suggests a qualitative difference between them and the other groups. The move from direct order to inverse order, from conservation of number to an intermediary stage, is accompanied by an important progress in the construction of seriation and greater flexibility in grouping objects.   Whilst the majority of children in the population studied were supposedly still dealing with topological structures which, in our choice of tests, have a privileged status, the children from privileged environments should, one supposes, have already mastered them, which would make it much easier for them to exhibit behaviour closer to the concrete operational stage.

1.3 Explanatory hypotheses

A finding of this kind leads us to consider the explanatory hypotheses most often proposed to account for differences linked with social status.   There are three types of hypothesis:

Hypothesis 1:   that the differences are merely an artefact of the testing situation.

Hypothesis 2:   that the differences are linked to characteristics peculiar to children from a socially and culturally deprived environment.

Hypothesis 3:   that the differences essentially reflect differences in the rhythms of development.

The first hypothesis raises several considerations:

(i)   The Piagetian tasks can be applied in such a way as to avoid the dangers of traditional psychometric testing, and to describe children from socially and culturally deprived environments in positive terms.   This attitude, which we shared at the outset of the research, renews the hope of developing democratic tests.   This notion, put forward by the Chicago school, is regarded by some research workers as Utopian and reformist.   In any case our results seem to show that the tests based on Piaget are no more socially egalitarian than are tests which purport to measure I.Q.

(ii) Developmental differences linked with social status do not so much affect the level of structurisation as the ways in which it comes about (1).   This position is coupled with criticism of tests: 'By their very construction, tests are linked with school success.   This is directly so simply because of their content, at least as far as tests of intelligence are concerned.   In a more subtle way this is true for the method of questioning used, which applies to all tests, even those which claim to be "non-verbal" or "independent of school learning".   In fact, the language used by the examiner, and that expected in reply, the authoritarian relationship between tester and tested, imply that the tests, like the school itself, are rooted in a certain form of culture and of social relationships.' (2)

(iii) Differences of achievement in tests, as in the school performance of children from working-class environments, cannot be interpreted in purely psychological terms.   The transformation of differences into deficits is a socio-political problem.   'In fact, no normal child is ever handicapped, but merely different from a reference group which holds the power.' (3)

Hypotheses 2 (deficits which can be attributed to the child and its family) and 3 (differences in rhythms of development) cannot be considered independently of the discussions raised by the first hypothesis.   Theories concerning deficits and differences in the rhythms of development would only be tenable if the differences observed were resistant to all forms of learning or social inter-action which aims to reduce them, and if the methods of utilisation, expression and appropriation of knowledge, the methods of social change, were not exclusively representative of a dominant culture.

The interpretation of our results is thus only valid in terms of the research methodology of which they were a product: a comparative and quantitative method applied to operational tests within the framework of a child-adult interaction suitable to a semi-structured clinical examination.

Nevertheless, differential study of this kind does not reveal characteristics peculiar to the group of working-class children.   On the contrary, the results suggest a difference in the rhythm of development in favour of children from privileged environments, and more particularly, calls in question Piaget's assumption that structurally equivalent notions are interdependent and simultaneous.   This is why it seems necessary both to check the validity of the Piagetian tests, the influence of the content, what can be observed and the systems of social relations which are implicit in the proposed tasks, as well as to lay bare the developmental sub-systems and the ways in which they correlate.

Without such knowledge, any interpretation of developmental differences linked with socio-cultural environment is in danger of going beyond the facts.   Such problems should be borne in mind in learning situations, i.e. situations involving behavioural change.   Because we were not able to control these numerous variables, we must be satisfied not to dissociate the findings of differential studies from the results of intervention in the nursery school.

It is not so much a question of denying the differences, but of how to account for the variability of behaviour linked with developmental structures, with their rhythm, their method of utilisation and expression, in relation both to the psycho-social and to the institutional context.   This, the problem facing the educational research worker, is the same as that facing the teacher: the provision of conditions which will facilitate the reorganisation of behaviour in terms of set objectives.

2. Action in the Nursery School

2.1 Analytical phase: providing an heuristic environment (1971-1972)

The urgency of certain problems (such as receiving two-year olds into day care, the high failure rate in the first year of primary school) led to a reorganisation and division of the work of the research workers.   Only one remained in the nursery school.   The teacher in the third year of the preschool who no longer wished to collaborate personally in the work, agreed to let us take care of the children in her class.   A trainee nursery teacher was engaged.   Since the new

classrooms were not yet available, a caravan was rented and installed opposite
the school.   Thus we were obliged to resign ourselves to a solution which we
had rejected at the outset of the project: conducting work parallel to that of
the class.

2.1.1 Objectives and procedure

Organisation of work in small groups: five groups each made up of five children
meeting twice weekly.

Each week, in collaboration with the preschool teacher, activities were trans-
lated into behavioural units defined along two dimensions:

- Content (social, physical, spatial-temporal and logico-mathematical knowledge,
  representational support: imitation, language, symbols, signs)
- Intellectual processes (reinforcement of the processes of anticipation and
  control of the action by the child)

We attempted to specify a repertoire of strategies corresponding to the particular needs of the children.   This is a question of organising optimal educational situations, i.e. of providing the most appropriate information for the
problem at issue and of structuring the child's activities.   Particular attention is given to how the child's success or failure is checked.   The feedback
should be as concrete as possible, i.e. related to the objects (the effects of
action and not words);   so far as social feedback is concerned, discussion with
peers is preferred to the verbal praise of the adult.   A non-random, structured
environment is organised not only by arranging the material, but by proposing
'language and social relations sufficiently formalised so that the child's
actions are clearly consistent or inconsistent with the rules'. (4)

Frequently teachers, in response to the children's behaviour, are inclined to
'exercise discipline'.   To get rid of this tendency, which involves either
drilling, or histrionics (capturing the attention of the children-spectators), we
'conditioned' the children to become autonomous.   The 'reinforcements' developed
from immediate and primary reward to a system in which tokens were given for
success in freely chosen activities, either individually or in small groups
(cooking, washing the dishes, listening to a story, reading, recording someone
else's (or one's own) voice, playing...).

Some activities were centred on individual needs (checking impulsiveness, getting
in the first blow in children used to defending themselves against being hit,
specific knowledge...).   The idea was that the child should fulfil the task set
him by the adult before he went to the activity chosen by himself.

2.1.2 Results and comments

Formative evaluation

The teacher and the research worker discussed both individual and group behaviour
observed in each unit that had been set up when the session was prepared so that
conditions for subsequent learning could be properly constructed.   At each
session, the teacher checked a specific aspect of the particular programme in
use, styles of thinking found in cognitive development, the specific knowledge
useful in carrying out other activities, or even the nature of the freely chosen
'reinforcements'.

In the course of the last sessions, intrinsic reinforcements took the place of
tokens and extrinsic reinforcements.   It is possible for several activities to
be carried out simultaneously without too much disorder.   The system used seems

pertinent to the extent that it favoured an organised way of living together, fostered autonomy, a respect for others' choices and it brought about a fairer relationship between children and adults.

Similarly, progress in cognitive skills was accompanied by other changes: the children dared to express their convictions, take the initiative, explore the equipment, rediscover symbolic play, broaden the field of expression...

Summative evaluation

Both at the beginning and at the end of the programme, tests of operations, verbal tests and a questionnaire concerning classroom attitudes were used. The results were compared with those achieved by children in the third kindergarten 'grade' (5-6 year olds) in the course of the preceding years.

Important progress was observed on all the tests of operations and particularly seriation construction: the range of scores on the different tests was very wide at the beginning, but much smaller towards the end of the project; the learning programme seems to have made the results more homogeneous. Each child showed development in every test.

For comparable tests, the picture of relative gains suggests results equal to or better than those attained in the course of the two preceding years. However, the relative gains vary according to the child's background. They confirm that the two groups of children develop in the same way, but they also indicate a systematic move towards the top of the scale in the case of children from average or privileged environments, who seem to have profited most from the intervention.

This 'behaviourist' phase of the work raises the problem of integrating behaviour modification techniques into a theory of development, and of how far this methodology is compatible with the more egalitarian and mutual relationships which should be established between all participants. As regards this second period of the research, one can really speak of cooperative activity. Admittedly, the research worker still proposes the model, but formative evaluation demands that the objectives and the control methods be continually discussed, specified, criticised and negotiated.

2.2 Phase of synthesis: combination of developmental and cultural aspects (1972-1974)

Circumstances forced us to make a new choice: either continue an action parallel to that of the teacher in school, or integrate our intervention into the classroom. This second possibility was more in line with our basic position. The first beneficial effect of introducing the teacher into a newly constituted class will be that the number of children per class will be reduced.

2.2.1 Objectives and procedure

The preschool teacher returned to a class and the usual ways of the nursery school, notably thematic work. The research worker, whose job was not to tell her how to go about her daily work, became a consultant. A meeting was held each fortnight.

Theoretical knowledge is a necessary but not sufficient prerequisite for apposite practice. The final phase of our work comes close to C. Kamii's recent conceptualisation of objectives which reflects a real integration of the socio-emotional and intellectual aspects of development (5).

Developmental aspect

- Establish relationships of equality between children, and a different relationship between children and adults (make the roles and rules explicit, vary the
  roles, make up the rules for oneself, give the children the chance to see
  things from another's viewpoint, to settle conflicts, to choose and decide...)
- Provide situations and equipment which encourage actions which produce interesting effects and have certain aims in mind (6).
- Within the context of these experiences meaningful for the child, organise
  feedback which is appropriate to what the class is learning, feedback about
  people (social knowledge), feedback from objects (knowledge of the physical
  world), the putting of questions and developing of social interactions which
  promote internal feedback (logico-mathematical knowledge).
- Foster successful behaviour at the pre-operational level, as a necessary
  prerequisite for fundamental operations (identity, functional relations,
  topological order...)

Cultural aspect

If learning only results from meaningful situations, it is essential to respect
the child's cultural identity and to acknowledge his own social and linguistic
experiences.

What are the values which underlie the activities, determine the rhythm and ritual
of life in class and in school, the system of rewards and punishments used, the
content of themes (the home, family, job, festivals)?   To what extent are these
values consistent or inconsistent with the family background?

Example: the fair: an occasion for symbolic games in the sandpit, the handling
           of money, tasting different things... an enjoyable or frightening
           experience... or an opportunity to think about how one enjoys oneself,
           how the relation between work and play (leisure) is viewed in different
           social environments.   To the teacher, children work as they play.
           They play 'seriously', but what does it mean to the parents, to the
           children?

This analysis induces teacher and research worker to get outside themselves, to
uncover the contradictions, particularly those brought about by personal values
and/or by institutional restrictions (7) and to open up a range of possibilities
which allow for personal choice.

The operationalisation of intermediate objectives demands an interplay between
theory and practice (why?) whilst the discussion of roles, rules, the content of
the themes, refers back to implicit cultural values and ideologies (why?).

2.2.2   Results and comments

Formative evaluation

From the beginning of the year, the children were allowed to conduct several
activities of their own choice at the same time.

Disciplinary standards were adjusted rather than changed (greater flexibility in
the rules, a dialogue with the nursery school teacher...).   The teacher
noticed children's initiatives, inventions, how mutually helpful or cooperative
the children were amongst themselves, but was also delighted if the pupils were
orderly, clean and polite ('They are the only ones who come to shake hands.').

Notes about the children's behaviour appeared regularly in the class log and
reflect a concern to adjust the level of difficulty, to encourage creative responses, to investigate whether or not pre-operational conduct has been achieved.

Differences between children were taken into account in a more positive way by
adjusting activities to the children's true potential, by concentrating on what
they might like, and be familiar with in terms of their family environment.

Collaboration began with the teacher from the parallel class (R) who drew her
inspiration from the activities, but put forward other ones.   Sometimes, shared
experiences were organised in which the children moved from one class to the
other.

Summative evaluation

An inclusion test and the Raven and Frostig tests were added to the Piagetian
tasks of the preceding years.   The results of class P were compared to those of
the parallel class (R), the one in which the teacher collaborated with P after
initially refusing to participate in the research.

It is interesting to note that the results of the two parallel clases showed a
tendency to converge in the course of the two years.   In view of the exchanges
which took place between the teachers, this could be explained in terms of a
positive 'spread'.   On the other hand, it could be related to the decrease in
the number of children per class.   However, this important factor does not
appear fully to account for the results, particularly those of class P.

The final year of the research was marked by less frequent contact between the
research worker and the teacher, who became increasingly independent in her work.
Nevertheless, the gain was maintained and in class P was inclined even to
increase.   Formative evaluation revealed that the teacher maintained and adapted
for her class some of the strategies developed in the analytical phase.

The change in results which came to light during the second period was once more
emphasised: an increase in the level of competence in the group and a reduction
on the range of individual results.   A third feature became evident, particularly in class P: that part of the variance linked with social status was clearly
reduced.   In this class, the relative gains of children from deprived environments even showed a tendency to be superior.

Progress in the matrices tests and the class inclusion tasks was modest, but the
large majority of children mastered tests characterised by spatial concepts and
qualitative logic, which only children from non-deprived environments mastered
in the differential studies.

This homogenisation of developmental rhythms coincides, on the one hand, with the
establishment in the context of experience meaningful to the child, of what may
well be the prerequisites for concrete operational thinking (identity, functional
relations, topological order...), and on the other, with the recognition of the
value of the social life of the class and a respect for the cultural identity of
the children.

It would probably not be going too far to see these as the beginnings of the
changes suitable to mastery learning, which will become much more apparent in
the work carried out in the first primary school year.

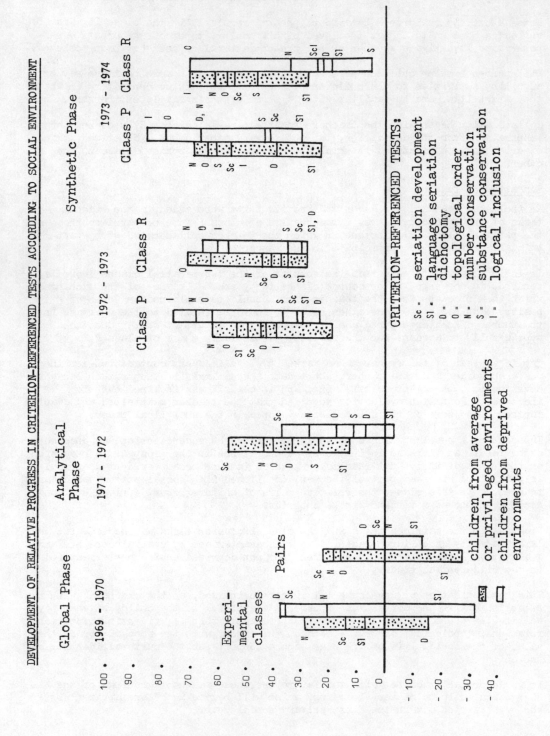

DEVELOPMENT OF RELATIVE PROGRESS IN CRITERION-REFERENCED TESTS ACCORDING TO SOCIAL ENVIRONMENT

CRITERION-REFERENCED TESTS:

Sc = seriation development
Sl = language seriation
D = dichotomy
O = topological order
N = number conservation
S = substance conservation
I = logical inclusion

2.2.3 <u>Conclusion</u>

A developmental theory such as that of Piaget provides a valuable conceptual framework for preschool intervention, provided that it is neither reduced to a juxtaposition of cognitive know-how nor adheres too exclusively to its instrumental aspect.   Undoubtedly, like others before us, we have used tests developed to solve certain theoretical questions, inappropriately either as diagnostic or differential tests, or as criterion tests.

In view of its constructive nature, this theory makes it possible to expose the empirical assumptions implicit in the teaching methods generally evident in the preschool (abstract notions put in concrete form in 'educative games', confusion between words and concepts, dissociation between content and process), practices which engender the 'school inadaptation' of children from a working-class environment.

Because the theory is interactionist it demands that there should be continuity between the child's pre- and out-of-school experiences and that we should recognise the child's cultural identity as a condition for the successful establishment of an heuristic environment.

The socio-emotional and cognitive aspects proved to be inseparable.   By stressing autonomy and more equal relationships among children, and with the adult, the teacher is led to be aware of the hidden curriculum and to bring about changes in the life of her class.   One criterion of success is that the teacher comes to use the proposed conceptual framework not only for the benefit of the children, or to please the research worker or the inspector, but as a working tool which will develop her own independence (to make assumptions, prove them to be right on the basis of actual class situations, acknowledge her own mistakes and modify her teaching and evaluation methods with full knowledge of the facts).   This kind of activity should be accompanied by a sharing of experiences.

Similarly, how can more equal relationships between children be established without sooner or later considering the relations between the adults and the school, and, in particular, between the teachers and the research workers? Action research changes social relations.

The major phases of the pre-school intervention programme are linked, on one hand with the change in the relation between theory and practice, and on the other, to the specific conditions encountered in the school in which the intervention programme took place.

We tried not to separate the measurement of the effects of the analysis of the educational practices from the implicit cultural values.   Our work also revealed the importance of the way in which intervention is set up and carried out.   It would have been better to have given a full account of these conditions (the effect of the school on society, family, trade unions, morphological, ecological and financial infra-structure...), which are more often than not passed over in silence or forgotten, but which are nonetheless necessary to an understanding of the outcomes of an action research project.   The psychological aspects of the intervention must of necessity be supplemented by sociological ones.   But if we wish to do this, we find that there is a paucity of intruments.   The sole evidence of change was the log book of the research.   We know now that the elaborated evaluation provides the research workers with less primitive tools!(8)

Having started out from the assumption that 'there is nothing as useful as a good theory', the complexity of an action research programme has now convinced us that it is truer to say that everyday practice needs a theory capable of explaining and changing it.

3. Action Research in the Field of Initial and Further Training of Nursery School Teachers (as from 1975)

A way has been found to continue the project.   The basic methodological options remain the same: field research with those directly concerned.   This project concretely initiates a policy which aims to bring about, within a centralised school system, 'research which does not simply retrain teachers to put into practice innovations devised by others, but makes them independent professionals with full responsibility'(9).   This work, which does not separate initial and further training of teachers, goes on simultaneously in pre-schools and teacher training colleges.

3.1   In the nursery school

In conjunction with a group of nursery school teachers, lecturers in education and nursery school inspectors, we are developing activities related to knowledge of the environment, which have proved to be particularly valuable in previous trials;   these activities cover different aspects of development - the socio-emotional, spatial-temporal, logico-mathematical spheres - and bring into play manual as well as intellectual skills, thus giving all children a chance.

This time, we did not start from a conceptual framework previously prepared by the research workers.   The procedure was as follows:

- Sharing experiences: the teachers presented and discussed activities based upon their own experience.

- Sharing information and reconstruction of a conceptual framework: the research workers provided the group with literature which made it possible to enlarge upon and clarify problems brought up when discussing concrete examples.

- Return to the practical: the teachers organised workshops.   The research workers video-recorded these attempts which were then discussed in the group.

- An attempt at synthesis.

These of course - in an accelerated form - are the stages which arose in the course of the previous programme.   The development of activities concerned with the environment was a valuable trigger.   Properly used such activities necessarily bring about a change in the organisation of the class, in the interactions among children, and between children and their teachers.   A number of the teachers trying to change their classes into class-workshops decided to collaborate and to create groups in which pre-school children could work with older children.   This modification was accompanied by a redefinition of both cognitive and affective objectives and a consideration of the school as an institution which puts limits on initiative.

3.2   In the teacher training college

Active methods in education suggest that, instead of directing the child's activity, the teacher should follow it while, nevertheless, controlling it by a suitable feedback.   The choice of this stance requires great flexibility from the teacher, and we suggest that student teachers could be trained for this during their initial teacher-education.

We have developed a programme (micro-teaching with the use of video-tape) which trains student teachers to individualise the education they give, and to adapt it to small groups of children.   This scheme seems useful in teaching them how to differentiate educational methods, and to get away from the cliches of explanatory judgement which have a tendency to label, value or denigrate children (he is 'dyslexic', 'deprived', 'individualistic', a 'good pupil') or worse, to accept conventional norms ('if you teach the whole class, you are sure that each child is getting the same thing').

Thanks to the micro-teaching, trainee teachers discover that the behaviour and attitudes of individual children are linked with teaching methods and institutional and social conditions.   By changing their own educational styles, they become aware of the norms implicit in their judgements and identify some of the processes which convert socio-cultural differences into school failure.

NOTES AND REFERENCES

(1) Breaute, M. et al., Essai d'étude comparative selon le milieu socio-culturel d'origine de l'acquisition de la notion d'équivalence numérique, in Travaux du C.R.E.S.A.S., no.6, 1972.

(2) Bresson, F. L'élimination par la psychologie, Le monde de l'Education, 4, 11, 1975.

(3) Landsheere, G. de, Handicapés ou differents? Bulletin d'Information, Conseil de l'Europe, 1, p.95.

(4) The theoretical hypotheses related to the qualities of an educationally stimulating environment are inspired by those defined by M. Reuchlin, in Les facteurs socio-economiques du développement cognitif, P.U.F., Paris, 1972, p.113

(5) Kamii, C., De Vries, R. Piaget for early education, in Parler, R.K. (Ed), The preschool in Action (second edition), Allyn and Bacon, Boston, 1974.

(6) 'It is true that the child, given the opportunity, can become interested in arranging things in series, in classifying things just for the sake of it, etc.   But, in broader terms, it is with regard to events or phenomena demanding clarification and objectives demanding attainment through causal arrangement that most use will be made of the operations.' (p.26) Piaget, J. and Gracia R. (1971) Les explications causales, P.U.F., Paris.

(7) For example, the physical conditions, the number of children reinforces the requirement of regularity, order and cleanliness.

(8) Thirion, A.M. Evaluation de la recherche-action, in Problèmes de l'évaluation dans l'éducation préscolaire. Conseil de l'Europe, Strasbourg, 1975.

(9) Vanbergen, P., Enseignement et recherche en Education, Revue de la Direction Générale de l'Organisation des Etudes, 8th year, no.10, December.

4 Mastery Learning in the First Year of Primary School

1. Changing the School

It is now commonplace to point to the ambiguity of the concept of compensatory education which distracts attention from the deficiencies in the school itself and focuses upon deficiencies within the community, family and child (1).   Socio-cultural differences do not automatically become scholastic differences;   a certain number of educational and institutional mechanisms intervene to cause precisely such a change.

These mechanisms appear clearly in the primary school and its curriculum.   One of the most influential of these is linked with the use of normative evaluation. This type of evaluation plays a selective role, on a psychological level, through screening which can lead to streaming (special education, and remedial classes) and, on an educational level, by causing failure and repetition of a year.   In addition, as C. Chiland notes, whether a given child goes to a remedial group or class or repeats a year is 'frequently not linked with educational considerations but with administrative or circumstantial ones'. (2)

Moreover, our research shows that the differences in quality of teaching, already revealed in international surveys, become marked at the very start of compulsory schooling and seriously hinder policies of democratisation.

1.1 Teaching of an unequal quality

Reading failure, to a large extent, determines failure in the first year of primary school.   To study this phenomenon more closely, we used a battery of tests predicting reading achievement.

From the results of a series of readiness tests, a profile of each child's likely achievement was drawn up, together with an upper and lower limit giving an 80 per cent chance of success.   Successive measures of 5-year old children in the last preschool year, taken in the course of the first part of the project, showed that after three, six, nine and twelve months of learning to read, the averages of the predicted scores differed according to social status (3).   This finding decided us to intervene in the first primary school year.   This began in the third year of the project.

Parallel to this action, the PREDIC method (4), applied to sixty-two classes

(1,156 children) showed great differences between classes in average achievement.
When related to the predictions, these differences allow us to estimate the
'handicap' (used here in the technical, sporting sense of the word, i.e. connoting
either advance or delay) which affects groups of pupils simply because they
attend a particular class rather than any other.   This is why we have attempted
to assess the 'weight' of <u>attending a specific class</u> (5) by introducing this
factor as an element in predicting the observed achievement in a multiple
regression analysis.   A regression equation is obtained which attributes a
constant to each class which should be added to the pupil's predicted result in
order to obtain the observed score.   These coefficients range from -13 to +14.
<u>The distribution of these class constants is normal</u>.

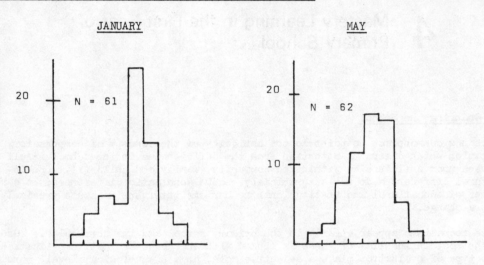

The higher this constant is, the more chance there is that initial aptitudes will
be realised and even surpassed.   In other words, being assigned to a given
class can increase or decrease a pupil's chance of success to a very great extent.

These results are strikingly reminiscent of the observations made in Belgium in
connection with international surveys organised by the International Association
for the Evaluation of School Achievement (I.E.A.).   In this country, at the end
of primary school, variables which relate to the academic year, the school and
the teacher account for a higher part of achievement variance than in other
industrialised countries.   It is thus apparent that school conditions and,
consequently, the quality of the teaching in Belgium vary greatly from class to
class.   The use of predictive reading readiness tests shows that this variability
is present at the beginning of compulsory schooling.

Equal success in school, not just simply equality of chance, presupposes a global
educational policy.   This general option would supposedly lead to three major
changes in the effects of schooling (6):

- Raising of the <u>average</u> level of attainment or competence at a given age.

- Reduction in the range of individual levels around the average (homogenization)

- A weakening of the statistical correlation between individual level and social
  origin.

2. <u>Meanwhile, Developing a Mastery Learning</u>

We chose to intervene in the first primary school year in a more specific and limited way than was the case in the pre-school.   The project, however, operated along the same lines.   We felt it unreasonable to regard learning difficulties, which are for the most part caused by teaching organisation and methods, as pathological disorders which call for specific treatment or remedial education. More than ever, the objective is to develop a genuine mastery learning situation, i.e. to make it possible for all pupils to master operationalised objectives. Teaching is so organised that each child progresses in different ways and at different rates.   The results of class learning are not normally distributed but take the form of a J-curve.

This form of organisation makes it necessary for the teacher to know the optimal stimulation level of each pupil.   Hence, the system of evaluation should conform to three prerequisites:

(i) Evaluation should be analytical. It is more important to determine precisely what a child can or cannot achieve than to give him a score.

(ii) Evaluation should be criterion-referenced (7).   Each child's performance is measured by progress along a sequence of attainments and not by comparison with the rest of the class or with a normative group.

(iii) Evaluation should be continuous and carried out during teaching.   It is complementary to the summative evaluation occurring at the end of each teaching unit in order to measure its effects.

When these three conditions are observed, evaluation becomes truly formative. It influences the definition of subsequent objectives and the way in which activities are conducted.   The utmost is done to make educational activity as suitable as possible to the individual child.

For such a system of evaluation to be practical, the teacher has to operational-ise objectives and specify the form of behaviour required from the pupil in the light of curriculum content (curriculum development).   Hence one seeks a true fit between objectives and curricular content on the one hand, and education on the other.

Mastery learning seems to be the only method of creating a truly individualised approach which nonetheless retains a group character in the current school system.

3. Methods of Action

There is a fundamental principle - an independent teacher should organise optimal teaching conditions for each pupil.   Thus it is not a matter of providing normative evaluation instruments applicable to absolutely any first year class, but of drawing up, in full cooperation with the teacher, a methodology for defin-ing objectives and the construction of an evaluation instrument to fit the given teaching programme.

So far, this method has been used in two first-year basic learning programmes - reading and mathematics.   For reading, the research workers concentrated on the system of evaluation.   In the case of mathematics, which implies a sequential organisation of a system of mental operations, the work was concerned with the definition of objectives, the content of the curriculum and the system of evaluation.   The successive stages can be outlined as follows.

3.1 Definition of increasingly specific objectives

- General objectives (broad intention)

- Terminal objectives in the first-year mathematical learning programme (seven teaching units)

- Specific objectives: the systematic combination of content and behaviour produces a model for the development of learning items (curriculum) and control (system of evaluation).

This procedure in fact leads to the development of a theoretical model of:

- the aspects which must be evaluated for each teaching unit;

- the potential range of these;

- and rules for the development of items.

The area to be dealt with can thus be defined in operational terms and it can be guaranteed that the items chosen to represent this content are as equivalent as possible.   However, this method is not sufficient to create a learning model. A model of this kind presupposes <u>statistical</u> validation (validity and simplification to essential factors), and <u>experimental</u> validation (the arrangement of categories in a learning hierarchy and a study of appropriate learning strategies for the pupils).   Standard psychometry is inadequate for these analyses.   It is essential to formulate a theory of reliability adequate to criterion-referenced tests, and a theory relating to the validity of the hierarchy of learning processes (8).

3.2 <u>Application of the evaluation system</u>

- Daily checks
- Periodic checks analysed from both class and individual points of view.

The results of the periodic checks conducted by the teacher were recorded on charts, in which the ordinate gives the names of the pupils and the abscissa the test items.

Three types of analysis are conducted.

(i)   A general analysis of class achievement in connection with the different items.

In the best conditions of achievement, each pupil should succeed in all the items generated from a topic taught in class.

A column by column consideration of the table of results shows whether or not the whole class has mastered a given concept.   The required level of achievement for a concept is dependent upon:

- its <u>complexity</u> in relation to the given educational level;

- its <u>importance</u> for the subsequent stages in the learning process.

It should be remarked that the determination of the minimum proportion of pupils who should master a concept before the class moves on to the next stage, is a limitation linked with class teaching: it disappears when teaching is individualised.

(ii)   An analysis of the achievements of any one child in the different items of a test.

The aim here is to estimate the <u>learning achievements of each child</u>, with a view to organising further teaching effectively.   This analysis also takes account

of general class performance.   The educational consequences of a child's insufficient mastery of a concept differ according to whether or not the concept has
been mastered by most of the class.   Sometimes it is necessary to offer individual remedial exercises; sometimes the matter must be presented in a different
way for the entire class.

(iii) An analysis of the development of attainment from one evaluation to the
      next.

A comparison of successive results in similar tests, in the course of different
evaluations, shows the child's progress in mathematics and reading.

Specific criteria determine whether or not there is:

- positive development or progress
- positive stability
- negative stability
- negative development or regression

3.3 Communicating findings to the teacher and discussion of methodological consequences

Mastery learning makes it essential for the teacher to draw all possible conclusions from the evaluation and to deal with each child in accordance with its needs.

The task is not easy.   It demands a fundamentally different form of class
organisation from that of frontal teaching aimed at the average.   It calls for
an entirely new repertory of teaching behaviour which has to be developed to
bring about a truly individual approach in teaching.

In the light of results from the tests, the research workers thus attempted to
find, with the teacher, exercises differentiated in accordance with the levels of
achievement observed in class.   The style of this procedure may appear, on first
impression, to be restrictive and incompatible with lively and functional teaching.
This however is by no means so, for the evaluation instruments do not dictate
teaching methods.   On the contrary, having been discussed and developed in
conjunction with the teachers themselves, they are closely adapted to the
initiatives taken by their instigators.

4. Results

Research in the field of reading was begun in 1971; research into mathematics
followed in 1972; both were conducted in the two first-year classes of a primary
school in a working-class district in the city of Liège.   These experimental
classes were compared to control classes of an equivalent socio-economic level.
As a result of requests from neighbouring districts, a number of groups was
added to those already mentioned.

The experimental design consisted of a system of internal evaluation (centred on
the development of the experimental groups) and a system of external evaluation
(founded on a comparison with the control group).   The project made it possible
to confirm the following operational hypotheses:

- Continuous, analytical and criterion-referenced evaluation makes it possible
  for the teacher to become aware of the difficulties encountered by children
  in the course of their learning.

- This awareness of the difficulties encourages her to adjust her teaching methods to suit both the group and the individual. These are the circumstances in which evaluation plays its truly formative role.

- Finally, this continual readjustment of teaching methods makes it possible for each child to achieve the specified criterion.

4.1 Internal evaluation

Formative evaluation, because of its analytical and criterion-referenced nature, makes it possible to follow the development of the process until key concepts have been mastered by most of the pupils.

Thus, the final summative evaluation in mathematics demonstrates knowledge of fundamental operations on the first twenty numbers.

Added to this continuous exhaustive assessment was a normative evaluation, made with the help of a reading test and a mathematics test. In each of these tests, the scores obtained at the end of the first year could be compared to the predicted scores. The latter had been established one year earlier, at the end of pre-school, with the help of prognostic batteries developed in the Laboratoire de Pédagogie expérimentale in Liège. Thanks to these instruments, we have at our disposal each child's probable learning curve. The difference between actual score and predicted score made it possible to evaluate the effectiveness of the intervening teaching (9). In the case of the experimental classes, the actual scores were always higher than the predicted scores, except in the case of a very small number of children, for whom teaching would have to be supplemented by thorough psychological help.

An analysis of the class log, class visits, reactions which arose during preparatory discussion sessions, provided proof of modifications in the behaviour of those teachers responsible for the experimental classes. The fact that they were anxious to vary the approach to concepts, to make more analytical, criterion-referenced evaluations, and to adapt teaching to the tempo of the children, showed that they had adopted the most important mastery learning strategies. But these new strategies presuppose, above all, a profound change of attitude. In the eyes of the teacher, each child should exist in its own right and thus benefit from her positive expectations.

However, even if teachers completely mastered the system of evaluation, they did not yet accept all its consequences, the most important of which would be to break the class into autonomous ability groups.

4.2 External evaluation

External evaluation confirmed the results of the internal evaluation. Standardised examinations organised by the city of Liège made it possible to compare the mathematical results of the first experimental class with a class identical to it both in numbers of pupils and in socio-economic background. For all the structures tested, the achievement of the experimental class was superior to that of the control class. Only very rare exceptions to this rule were found. The difference widened particularly with exercises involving an unfamiliar structure, which demand greater flexibility and reversibility of thought on the part of the child.

In addition, actual and predicted scores were compared in experimental and control groups. The experimental classes which had a predicted average equal to

that of the control groups made the most important gain.   The results were
clearly better than the predictions.

The results were not only <u>superior</u>, but they revealed a far greater degree of
<u>homogeneity</u>, as compared with the control classes, where the differences between
children tended to increase and where weak and strong groups formed which
diverged more and more throughout the year.

By way of example, the following diagrams illustrate the reading results obtained.
The scatter plots were established on the basis of predicted performance (10), in
abscissa, and obtained performance (11), in ordinate.

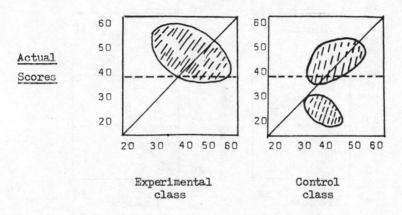

Predicted scores

Actual Scores

Experimental class   Control class

Points which fall on the diagonal line of the graph indicate that prediction has
been exact.   Points above the diagonal line indicate performances which are
higher than predicted.   Points below the diagonal represent performances inferior
to the predicted performance.

The results were analysed by <u>socio-economic status</u>.   Three groups were established by combining the occupational and educational levels of the parents: deprived
(D), average (A) and privileged (P) (12).   Because of the working-class
environment in which the project was conducted, the three socio-economic levels
are unequally represented.

The following graphs compare actual scores with the predicted scores in reading
ability, in the course of the academic year 1970-1971 (when intervention did not
take place) and during the year 1971-1972 (when it did), in the working-class
environment.   Only the average scores of the three groups of children have been
recorded on the graphs which illustrate development after six and nine month
periods of learning.

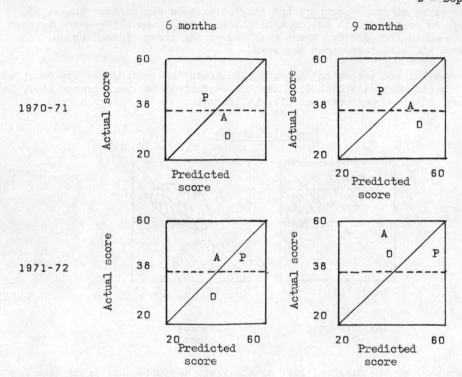

In 1970-1971, the results after six months (which were disastrous for the deprived children) remained that way after nine months of learning.   By way of contrast, thanks to the 1971-1972 project, the results of the deprived children after six months, while not excellent, showed definite progress in comparison with the preceding year.   And - most important of all - this progress was corroborated at nine months, in that the average results of deprived children attained those of the privileged children, which is above the desired minimum (38 points).   Although it is the deprived children who reap the greatest profits from the project which was undertaken, the project was clearly profitable for all.

Generally speaking, the results of both internal and external evaluations reflect the same trends:

- a rise in average score

- reduced variation between individuals (homogeneity)

- a weakening of the statistical relation between individual levels of achievement and social origins.

5.   The Limitations of Mastery Learning

Our procedure is only a very incomplete answer to the demands of mastery learning, which aims to allow each child to progress in different ways and at a different pace.   The traditional classroom is a strait jacket which forbids variations in the time taken.   The formulae which would make flexibility possible (individual work, specific ability grouping, etc.) are well known, but they have not yet been put into practice. The educational structure and teaching methods must be questioned. 'The use of homogeneous groups can only be effective if teachers vary their strategies in terms of the groups, and are not satisfied merely to modify their demands without any other change.' (13)

To the limitations of school system itself and of the way teachers are trained, the particular limitations of mastery learning itself are added. It raises many conceptual and methodological problems (definition and hierarchical arrangement of teaching units, relation between content and learning process, statistics of criterion-referenced tests, etc.) that have frequently been sidestepped or dealt with unsatisfactorily, and which can make this system appear to be an over-simplification of teaching-learning processes.

The organisation and structure of education represent only one area for possible changes. If we are to bring about radical change another significant aspect must emerge; that of the cultural contexts of learning. Only when these two aspects are integrated, something we have not as yet been able to do, can the concept of 'compensatory education' be truly left behind.

6. The Advantages of Mastery Learning

Despite its serious limitations, mastery learning does seem to provide a partial but relatively successful solution to the debate on equality in the eyes of the school. It is a sophisticated tool which could contribute to the 'loss of innocence in education'(14). Its application brings a levelling upwards and begins a process of change truly characteristic of a real attempt to democratise elementary education (15). It breaks the process causing school failure. It 'depathologises' failure and 'allows a clear distinction to be made of those difficulties in learning which require examination in depth and special treatment'. (16)

The teacher-pupil relationship is an important element in mastery learning. We have been able to observe, and hope in the future to analyse more explicitly, teacher expectation of the child's potential.

Instruments to evaluate objectives have been developed in conjunction with teachers; thus the latter have at their disposal a means of self-evaluation which promotes their autonomy.

7. Attempts at Dissemination of Mastery Learning to Other Schools

The mastery learning experiment described above has had two complementary extensions. In the case of reading, the approach is extensive. Many teachers are undertaking formative educational procedures along lines defined by a research centre, and which bear on the entire programme. In the case of mathematics, the approach is, on the other hand, intensive; here, a limited number of teachers are taking part in the development and trial of less extensive teaching modules. Each stage of the procedure is worked out in detail: definition of the objectives and their arrangement in order of importance, the development of analytical, formative and summative evaluation instruments, programming the activities in relation to the differentiated and successive levels of mastery.

7.1 Dissemination in the field of mathematics

The procedure adopted was two pronged: experimental validation of the analysis of objectives and of the instruments designed to measure their achievement; and training the teachers to evaluate systematically their own teaching.

<u>The first objective: experimental validation of the analyses of objectives</u>

A study of a number of essential points was found to be preferable to a general analysis of the entire mathematical programme in the first year of primary school.   These points were: intersectional relation, equivalent relation, representation on a plane of concrete reality, translation of verbal problems into equations.

Each item was analysed in accordance with the following stages:

(i)   Definition of the terminal objective

(ii)   The breakdown of this objective into items of content and the behavioural strategies to be shown by the pupil.

       These two analyses led to the definition of a large range of operational objectives.

(iii) Arrangement of these operational objectives in hierarchic order (importance and difficulty)

(iv)   Devising of an analytic pretest to determine the best point of entry for each individual or group of individuals to the learning sequence.

(v)   Devising formative instruments to check the level of achievement at each stage in the learning task.

(vi)   Development of a summative test.

In the first stage, the learning modules developed on the basis of this model can be used by the teachers, provided they are adapted to the class situation. In the second, teachers will develop other learning modules in collaboration with the research workers, one of the most important objectives of the entire project. Teachers bring their class experience; they know their pupils' potential, sometimes they have been using particular methods of their own, they are familiar with class teaching, and so on.   In addition, they take part in the field trials of the new instruments and suggest modifications, if necessary.   The research workers make the teachers familiar with systematic evaluation of given objectives, and thus guarantee an increased validity.   They arrange for the experimental testing of the learning sequences and the statistical analysis.

In more general terms, the research described here aims to train teachers in a scientific methodology of educational intervention.

<u>Second objective: training teachers to evaluate their own teaching systematically</u>

Participating in action research acts as a refresher course for teachers.   The benefits are twofold.   On the one hand, operational definition and arrangement of objectives in order of importance provides a guideline for choosing teaching activities; when the teacher proposes an exercise to her pupils, she is fully aware of the aims she is pursuing, of the possible extensions and variations of the exercise and what the relation is between the new learning and previous acquisitions.   On the other hand, the constant care to evaluate achievement by using instruments appropriate to the type of instruction guarantees that information necessary to organise individual or semi-individual instruction will be obtained.   Thus the conditions of mastery learning are brought into effect.

7.2 Dissemination in the field of reading

In the case of the team of research workers concerned with reading, the project centred mainly on the teacher's assessment of her pupils' achievements, and consequently of her own teaching.   Research workers and teachers together analysed the objectives, the form teaching should take and ways of evaluating whether they have been achieved by pupils.   In view of the fact that formative evaluation bears on results and not on teaching methods, teachers are free to choose their own teaching methods.   The teacher's success is linked with her 'educational well-being': successful instruction is partly determined by the impression a teacher gives of psychological security.   This is why it is so important not to influence the teacher's choice of method for teaching children to read.   It is up to the teacher to determine her objectives for the year, which way she should go to help her pupils achieve reading proficiency, and what individual remedial action can be taken in the event of difficulties.

The continuous assessment procedure demanded that the teacher check every six weeks what had been taught.   The university team analyzed these results, as much from the point of view of <u>quality</u> (measured content, the behaviour expected from the child...) as of <u>form</u> (how the exercises were put forward, how explicit the question was, how many questions there were...).

Seminars at which some twenty people were present (research workers, teachers, psychologists, training college lecturers in French and education, first and second year primary teachers and teachers from remedial classes) discussed the individual reports as well as more theoretical considerations, about the teacher's assessment of both her instruction and herself.

At the end of the year, the teacher, with the help of the psychologist who observed the children of her class, compiled the correlations between predicted and actual scores for each of her pupils, and assessed the productiveness of her own teaching.   In short, it involved the teacher assuming almost total responsibility for herself and for the assessment of the effectiveness of her teaching.

Conclusion

This operation created mutual understanding between teacher and psychologist, who discussed the problems the teacher encountered in class, and not only pupils' individual difficulties.

A similar project was undertaken with teachers in training in State teacher-training colleges, with a view to prevention rather than cure!   Work related to more limited objectives (in teaching practice carried out by students in the classroom) brought about fruitful exchanges between inspectors, lecturers, teachers of the mother tongue, student teachers and teaching practice supervisors.

The teachers met (with or without the inspector) and established their educational independence.   This is perhsps one of the most positive aspects of dissemination, and indicates the beginning of a group of pioneer teachers who will lead teams to enliven education.

NOTES AND REFERENCES

(1)   Bernstein, B., A Critique of the Concept of Compensatory Education, in
      Class, Codes and Control, Routledge and Kegan, London, 1971, p.193.

(2)   Chiland, C. (1971) L'enfant de 6 ans et son avenir, P.U.F., Paris, p.269.

(3)   Leclercq-Boxus, E. Etude differentielle de la prediction du rendement en
      lecture en première année primaire, in Recherche en Education, Recherches
      sur les handicaps socio-culturels de 0 à 7-8 ans. Bruxelles, Ministère de
      l'Education nationale et de la Culture française. 1973, pp.208-209.

(4)   PREDIC method.   This is an instrument devised by E. Leclercq-Boxus intended
      to predict the likelihood of success in the early learning of reading and
      thus to prevent failure in the first year.
      The results are given in the form of a record given to the teacher when the
      child begins school.   For each child this record gives:
        - a synthesis of test results
        - the probable learning profile
        - and an indication of a ± 10% margin of error

(5)   Two types of factors are thus taken into account: those related to the
      teacher (her educational qualifications, her professional consciousness, etc)
      and those related to the class situation (absence or replacement of teacher,
      epidemics, school atmosphere, etc.).

(6)   Perrenoud, P., Compensatory education and perpetuation of social classes,
      Outline of a political sociology for the democratisation of education.
      Information Bulletin, Conseil de l'Europe, April 1974, p.75.

(7)   We are concerned here with evaluation directed to the attainment of
      objectives (criterion-referenced evaluation) using tests related to a
      universe (universal defined tests).

(8)   Tourneur, Y., Application d'indices et de tests statistiques à l'évaluation
      de maîtrise. Colloque de l'Association Internationale de Pédagogie
      experimentale de Langue Française, Louvain.

(9)   The predictive instrument used for reading is already operational (Leclercq-
      Boxus, 1971).   The predictive test for mathematical achievement used in
      research described was still in its exploratory stage (Marcotty, 1972).
      R. de Bal and J. Paquay-Beckers have continued work on this test in the
      Laboratoire Experimentale de Pedagogie in the University of Liège.

(10) Leclercq-Boxus, E., op.cit., 1971.

(11) Inizan, A. (1964) Le temps d'apprendre à lire. Bourrelier, Paris.

(12) Deprived (D) - Primary and vocational education - unskilled workers,
                     unemployed, etc.
      Average (A) - Secondary school education; skilled workers, clerks, small
                     shopkeepers etc.
      Privileged(P)- Further and higher education; executives, teachers, etc.

(13) De Landsheere, G. (1974) Evaluation et examens, Précis de docimologie.
      F. Nathan, Paris; Labor, Bruxelles, 3rd edition, p.229.

(14) Bloom, B.S., Innocence in education. <u>The University of Chicago School Review</u>, <u>80</u>, No.3, May 1972.

(15) Perrenoud, P. op.cit.

(16) Chiland, C. op.cit.

Conclusions

A. <u>The conceptual and methodological analysis of the comparative and differential studies led to the need to analyse the processes of development and learning and their interaction with the school environment</u> (proximal and distal variables).

In short or medium term interventions, we must identify the educational and institutional mechanisms which turn socio-cultural differences into retardation and school failure.

Throughout the research, the facts constantly laid bare these processes:

- Segregation affecting the youngest working-class children begins before the school is legally able to receive them.

- The use of the pre-school (age of entry, attendance at crèches and making use of the school canteen) varies according to social status.

- The school tends to reinforce differences between boys and girls, to distinguish 'good' pupils from 'bad' ones, 'privileged' from 'deprived' children, the more effectively because it is done by the 'hidden' curriculum.

- Unequal standards of teaching in this country, grimly brought to light by international surveys (I.E.A.), are marked at the very start of compulsory schooling and seriously prejudice attempts at democratisation of education.

These findings suggest that any attempts at reform must take into consideration not only individual aspects but also and above all, contextual and institutional variables, the quality of school life.

B. <u>It is important to develop educational practices, at all levels of the school system, which neither select nor segregate.</u>

For the idea of compensatory education we have substituted that of mastery learning integrated with the social context. This choice makes two demands:

- a guarantee to all children of the right and means to acquire the basic skills;

- respect for the children's cultural identity, an acknowledgement that their

social and linguistic experiences are significant and valid for
changing the culture of the school.

This second demand is the one least effectively met. It is not enough
simply to define objectives; it is essential to detect the nature of the
obstacles (lack of adequate methodology, the research workers' own social
status, institutional rigidities, etc.).

Despite these serious limitations, the results of pre-school and primary
school intervention are, we think, important.

The changes brought about are typical of a scheme of real democratisation.
The methodology seems to us valid since it proved effective in breaking with
school failure.

The relevance of this instrumental change was further justified by the
change in attitude in children, teachers and research workers.   Theory and
technology were no longer the exclusive property of the scientific team; a
sharing of knowledge was born!

However, any short-term experiment, particularly when it is of a technical
nature, is often evanescent if not built into a more extensive scheme to
fight school failure.   In a centralised system, action research results run
the risk of being presented as finished products, which can be spread by
simple administrative action.   Another danger, in the present case, is that
of separating predictive instruments from mastery learning and of thus
reintroducing arbitrary early screening.

We feel that the dissemination of mastery learning is only relevant if it
adheres to the basic methodological choice - that of working in the field
with those concerned - and if it is integrated into initial teacher-training
as it was in our attempt at dissemination.

To say that more children should be able to acquire basic skills will not
change the situation if, at the same time, teachers are not given the means
and working conditions to enable them to do it.   Teachers should have at
their disposal not only techniques, but the means of analysing and checking
so that they understand how educational choices tie in with socio-political
decisions.

This poses the problem of educational policy itself, of the 'how' and 'why'
of school reforms.

C. It is important to link educational and social factors.

In our work, the link between educational and social factors was made both
inside the school and outside it.

Intervention in pre-school showed that teachers and research workers moved
from the strictly educational 'how' to the 'why', and asked questions about
the social function of the school.   Here we observe a breaking of the
barrier around knowledge to make it more generally available.   The accounts
of children's behaviour, the individual and interpersonal experiences of the
teachers were brought into relation with the features of the school and
social factors.

Criteria legitimising action research are different: solidarity instead of
judgements of value, new educational practices, spontaneous self-organised

groups, action through trade unions... The point is to find answers to the problems of everyday life and not to become involved in 'persuasive' political discussions or to provoke conflicts of opinion which block progress or arouse guilt feelings which inhibit action.

Action research consequently emerges both as a scientific and as a social exercise which presents fundamentally new conceptual, methodological and deontological problems. It offers the research worker the chance to get inside another's viewpoint, a new source of knowledge demanding that he produce methods adapted to the real and concrete conditions of his scientific practice.

Action research requires analysis of groups (interpersonal relationships), organisation (adjustment of means to fixed objectives) and institutions (socio-political determinants). The combination of these different analyses makes it possible to make action effective, deal with conflicts, to place oneself in an understandable play of forces.

Cooperation with popular education movements brings us into contact with parents, not in the family context, but in the context of groups striving for social reforms.

In uch situations, the point is not merely to minimise the consequences of socio-cultural inequality, but to examine their causes. Consequently, what is at stake in action research is, within a strongly structured and regulated educational and social context, to create conditions favourable to the unity and continuity of education, and which make it possible for those directly involved to take an active part in defining and achieving objectives.

According to sociologists like A. Touraine, our current industrialised society is becoming a programmed society. This emerging society has the power to act, be it directly or indirectly, not only on production, but also on consumption, leisure time, education and habitat. The management structure inherent in this social change becomes the new stake in dealings between the social classes.

Whether in the family, school, local community school, popular education or any other imaginable context, the matter in hand is to promote new social practices which encourage working-class adults and children to be the instigators of their own development and partners in a more just society, in which the relationships of dominance and power between social groups will be modified.

Part 4
Education and Social Environment

Summary of the research undertaken by the Departement des
Etudes et des Recherches Psycho-pédagogiques de l'Université
de l'Etat à Mons

Prof. Jean Burion
Jean-Pierre Pourtois
Jean Auverdin
Huguette Desmet
Nicole Druart
José Menu

Introduction

The research project was carried out by a team from the Department of Educational Studies in the State University of Mons. It was supported by a grant from the Bernard van Leer Foundation. Its main objective was to discover those features of the environment which impede the educational progress of children between 3 and 8 years of age, and to develop the most effective educational methods and activities to overcome their effects. The final results were to be based on an objective evaluation of project data.

The target population consisted of 540 nuclear families, including both Belgian and foreign nationals, living in the economically, socially and culturally deprived region of the Borinage.

The investigations and activities of the project involved social groups in three different settings: the family, the school and the community.

The project was carried out in three phases:

Phase one: arousing awareness (October 1969 - September 1971)

Phase two: learning to participate (October 1971 - September 1973)

Phase three: learning to cooperate (October 1973 - September 1975)

In the course of each phase, interim reports describing the activities of the project were prepared. A list of these can be found in the appendix, and the numbers of the reports are indicated in the head of the sections that follow. Also specimen pages of the documents produced in each phase of the project are given.

1 The Environment

1. Geographical and Economic Context

The once thriving region of Le Hainaut has experienced a progressive decline in prosperity; this is particularly the case in Quaregnon, Frameries, Flénu and Cuesmes, all situated in the heart of the Borinage.

Mons is the administrative centre of this region. For many generations, Mons and its environs have provided employment for the majority of its population. Today, the collieries are for economic reasons closed down, and this has resulted in the impoverishment of the region. Many people have had to seek employment elsewhere; others have joined the ever-increasing ranks of the unemployed.

Attempts are being made to establish a number of new industries - but without much success. Consequently, a considerable percentage of the population is forced to work outside the region. Unemployment is estimated to be in excess of 22 per cent.

Another important problem is the immigrants - Italians, Spaniards, Greeks and Turks - who have settled in the Borinage since 1945, and who have been faced with a number of social, employment and cultural difficulties.

2. Cultural and Educational Context

Today education is seen increasingly as an indispensable investment in development. The results of a recent UNESCO survey (1) of school failure confirm our own observations.

The difficulties encountered by socially deprived children in adapting to the environment of present-day schools are well known. The lack of contact between parents and teachers frequently results in mutual ignorance and lack of understanding of the needs and rights of people and of communities.

Today it is accepted that the first years of life are the most important and the most formative, and there is a considerable body of evidence to show that early childhood has a determining influence on an individual's entire future (2).

From these earliest years inequality of opportunity is apparent. We have established that in the regions of the Borinage and the Centre 27.7 per cent of children fail in their first year of compulsory schooling (3). Furthermore, we find that 21 per cent of 5-year-old children are potential failures in reading. The social environment of these children can be classified as follows:

- well-to-do or affluent : 7.7%
- average : 17%
- poor or needy : 50%

NOTES AND REFERENCES

(1) UNESCO, (1970) Report of the 32nd Session of the International Conference. Geneva.

(2) Conseil de l'Europe. Politique de recherche éducationelle dans les pays européens. Survey 1973, p.43.

(3) This figure is based on an analysis of the school records of 845 children from 56 primary school classes who completed their first year of school on June 30th 1974.

2 The Research Project - Phase One: Arousing Awareness

1. Characteristics of the Socio-economic and Cultural Environment (Report No.1)

1.1 Special features of the environment

The deprived child cannot be considered apart from the social and environmental context in which he lives. He is in fact the product or victim of society, neighbourhood and family. The deprived child is thus defined in terms of the socio-economic and cultural characteristics of both his family and his social environment.

In the Borinage as elsewhere, social deprivation is not only linked with occupation, income, and the quality of housing, but also with a network of factors, such as poverty of cultural activity, the level of the parents' aspirations and their indifference to the problems of education. Which factors should be considered in defining the term 'social deprivation'?

1.2 Defining social status

A family's social environment was described by means of L'Indice Global de Désavantage Relatif (I.G.D.R.). This procedure is based on five social indicators:

- the occupation and resources of the parents
- the housing conditions
- the education level of the parents
- the cultural level of the family
- the parents' interest in the school and in the health of the child.

2. Pre-school Education for Socially Deprived Children

Having ascertained that the failure rate of deprived children is greater than that of children from more privileged social classes, and that 'social pressures' have inevitable consequences on the child's level of educational attainment, the team from Mons concentrated on the development of a range of preventative measures.

In our initial analysis, we described the more extreme aspects of social deprivation in the Borinage. In addition to the less than encouraging socio-economic living conditions, the disadvantage suffered by these families is clearly determined by the character of their cultural environment: by the low educational level of the parents, and the low level of cultural stimulation resulting from their impoverished material conditions.

We therefore concluded that it was essential to discover the most effective forms of educational innovation for use in the battle against such disadvantage, against the often hidden causes as well as the immediately obvious effects.

It became vitally important to establish educational methods designed to prevent intellectual and social backwardness of cultural origin. An educational research project was established to effect change on three levels: that of the child, the school and the parents.

From the main experimental methods examined, we derived the following list:

- special educational help given by a visiting remedial teacher
- meetings with parents
- educational pamphlets
- boxes of slides
- books to read at home
- consultations with an educational psychologist

The use of these educational methods helps to extend the pre-schools' present educational horizon by making it into a school for parents as well. In this whole area the basic contribution of this research depends on a programmed, controlled innovation.

Although it is essential to evaluate the results, to do so is both difficult and complicated. The analysis of the results gives rise to a consideration of and suggestions on the following:

- further training of pre-school teachers, their competence and commitment to their work;
- early and systematic identification of socio-emotional and cognitive deficit in the deprived child;
- educational intervention to make up for lack of cultural stimulation;
- differentiated roles of the pre-school, which aims to provide equality of opportunity for the children;
- the provision of individual activities relevant to the needs of each child;
- linguistic expression accompanying the child's handling of objects;
- school as a centre to train adults in family education;
- continuous observation of and individual help to be given to any child in serious difficulties.

However, direct help by the school given to the deprived child is not in itself sufficient. Intervention at family level is essential.

3. <u>An Attempt to give Educational Help to Socially Deprived Families</u> (Report No.2)

In this part of the research, we drew the attention of parents from socially deprived classes to their role as educators, and suggested to them changes of attitudes likely to stimulate the development of their child.

Five important educational factors distinguish socially privileged from socially deprived groups:

- the quality of the cultural and material environment of the child
- the readiness of the parents to contribute to the cultural development of their children
- the level of the parents' expectations for their children
- the interest shown by the parents in the school
- parental authority and the level of cooperation of parents and school.

These findings determined the orientation of the programme and the choice of steps to be taken.

The interventions took place in the homes of the socially deprived families. Altogether, 102 visits lasting 45 to 90 minutes each were made. The educational themes developed dealt with language, social relations, motor coordination, cognitive development and creativity. The parents played an active part in the search for techniques and situations which would bring about specific learning in each of the areas mentioned.

After the experiment we recorded changes in the following:

(a) the quality of the child's cultural and material environment:
  - availability of reading material
  - the cultural quality of the books made available to the children
  - the opportunities given to the child to play with water, sand and soil...

(b) the readiness of the parents to help their children educationally

(c) the interest shown by parents in the school work of their children

This experiment shows that educational help given to deprived families is effective provided that it focuses on specific educational components such as educational equipment, reference books, drawings, helping in the home. All suggestions for ways in which a child can be helped must be practical - short illustrated pamphlets, slides, direct observation of their children. It would seem that parents are mainly worried about 'how to do it' and seldom want to know why. Indeed most parents showed considerable dependence on the research worker.

4. A Child's Right to Education   (Report No.3)

4.1 Educational pamphlets

When dealing with people from a socially deprived environment, educational information must deal with practical situations and be expressed in simple, explicit language which helps to motivate the reader. To this end educational pamphlets were devised, to help in communicating to the parents the educational principles likely to help them to understand the importance of early childhood education.

The comic-strip technique in which each small section of text is supported by pictures, was used. This technique intrigues both the parents and the child, who can then colour in the pictures. Three pamphlets have been made:
(1) The young child's right to education
(2) Let's give them educational toys
(3) Your child at five

4.2 What parents think about the child's right to education

A special survey revealed the opinions and attitudes of parents in relation to
ten educational principles which, among others, were discussed and illustrated
in the pamphlet entitled 'The Young Child's Right to Education'.   Four thousand
copies of this were printed and given free to the families.   A questionnaire was
constructed to gather parents' opinions and attitudes to certain educational
problems.   We analysed the replies of the 200 families who agreed to take part
in this experiment.

- The content and illustrations of the pamphlet interested 8 out of 10 people.
  One out of every two people remembered particular notions, especially those
  concerned with the freedom of the child, with how much time parents make
  available to their children, and with the influence of home on the development
  of the child.

- 'A child must be aware of his parents' love'.   Nine out of ten parents
  thought they should so plan their day as to give the child real and sufficient
  attention.

- Of course the child should not be the centre of the universe: we should also
  foster his independence by giving him some space of his own.   The parents
  were aware of this, and in nine cases out of ten agreed with us on this point.

- 'Are good toys expensive?'   This question, illustrated in the handbook, was
  interpreted in various ways.   If we take the viewpoint that toys need not
  necessarily be bought and that any child can find in his own environment
  materials which can be used as toys, then suitable toys need not necessarily
  be expensive.   Parents in unskilled occupations and mothers who did not go
  out to work expressed a variety of opinions on this point.   Generally,
  however, they felt that educational toys are very expensive.

- 'The child should be allowed to draw, paint or make models, and full
  consideration should be given to what he wants to do'.   Similarly, 'the child's
  own interests should be encouraged and he should come to depend less and less
  on adults'.   Here not all parents were in agreement with us.   Some
  considered that the child will always need his parents and that he should not
  be encouraged to become emotionally detached from them.

- The most striking difference of opinion amongst parents emerges when it is
  suggested that they should 'leave a basket of fruit within easy reach of the
  child'.   One out of every two mothers who do not go out to work disagrees,
  while other parents see this as 'an opportunity for the child to exercise
  self-restraint'.

- It is with regard to independence and autonomy that differences between social
  groups emerge most clearly.   Middle or upper-middle class families favour
  early autonomous behaviour, whereas in lower social groups the mothers prolong
  the period during which their children are wholly dependent on them and the
  home.

- Five major elements make up a true adult education:
  (i)   enabling parents to understand the meaning of education in a general
         sense.
  (ii)   emphasising the main conditions likely to promote the child's develop-
         ment.
  (iii) emphasising the part played by relationships within the family.
  (iv)   analysing the role and nature of parental authority.
  (v)   ensuring that educational principles are accessible to all, and
         describing these in practical terms, in keeping with the experience of
         each individual.

- It is not only adolescents of both sexes who should be informed; it is equally essential that parents and adults who will be future parents should be better prepared to assume their role as educators.

Specimen pages from the pamphlet 'The Young Child's Right to Education'

The example you set is very important and it will shape the life and future of your children.

The quality of the examples mother gives influences the child's developing personality.

A child's relationship with his father allows him to experience more vigorous physical activity.

... the child acquires new ideas about balance, health, money
and many other aspects of life which we take for granted.

A variety of simple and inexpensive materials is necessary
for imitative games.

Familiar items such as pencils, biros and felt tips are very
useful in the child's work.

3 Phase Two: Learning to Participate

1. Educational Practices (Report No.4)

1.1 Presentation and content

We were concerned to find out more about the educational techniques which might be practised in the home. How do parents bring up their children? What are their opinions of, their attitudes and their reactions to the learning situations which all parents must encounter?

To answer these questions we used the 'critical incidents' technique and, with the help of slides, we presented mothers with situations in which the child is playing a specific role; for example, climbing a wall, taking a bicycle to pieces, playing at doctors, or exploring objects in a cupboard. The parents were invited to comment on a similar situation involving them at home. The comments were recorded in accordance with the six following themes:

Games related to vocations
    (a) nurse   (b) shopkeeper

Experimentation
    (a) mending things   (b) water play

Games that are not allowed
    (a) exploring   (b) climbing

1.2 Objectives

The impact of experiences within the family on the development of the child is important. There are, of course, many ways to bring up a child. This is why we presented a sample of parental attitudes to a specific activity involving the child; and we considered that the various comments of the mothers were indicative of their own educational practices. By reading the examples from them, either parents would be made aware of their own opinions or they would challenge the comments made. In this way we hoped to encourage each of them to learn from the experience of others.

2. Relationship between Aspects of the Personality of the Parents and the Kind of Educational Help Given (Report No.4)

The purpose of this analysis was to bring out certain peculiarities in the personalities of socially deprived parents as reflected in the Rorschach test, in order to discover the most appropriate types of psychological and educational help to be given to parents in socially deprived environments.   The study showed that:

- in general, parents have very limited cultural potential and deal with situations in a global way, without the ability to deal intellectually with the elements of which they are composed;

- the tendency to deal with problems superficially causes them to be passive in the face of events;

- their lack of creativity seems to be linked to their limited capacity to internalise or defer action;

- as a result, the ability to anticipate events by reflecting on their outcome, gives way to an attitude of uncritical acceptance;

- although they are quite capable of cooperative participation, they show little inclination to resolve difficulties by themselves;

- the lack of originality or individual thinking makes for conformity and contributes to their over-dependence on others to solve problems;

- their receptive attitudes are revealed by an excessive concern with conformity, conferring on them a considerable degree of social adaptation;

- this social adaptation leaves them open to suggestibility, which in turn partly accounts for their non-aggressive tendencies;

- when faced with a situation involving psychological stress, the ensuing reaction is one of rigidity and intolerance;

- there is a strong tendency to avoid entering into conflict with external reality;

- the lack of ambition makes them accept the uncertainties of life without question;

- able to get through life because of their capacity to adapt to external reality in a humdrum manner, most subjects nonetheless reveal somewhat limited emotional maturity.   This explains their somewhat precarious independence as well as their inability to form deep human relationships;

- although at home in concrete, tangible situations, their social relationships are marked by a lack of ego-differentiation;

- relationships are seldom personal, and the interests of the community are extremely limited socially: they would benefit from being enriched and diversified.

(a)   It is thus expedient to help such parents to become more aware of the important educational role they are called upon to play in bringing up their young children.   From the very first meetings with the parents the persuasive approach was used.   This approach takes into account the parents' tendency to be superficial in their consideration of problems, and puts them on their guard against that unquestioning passivity in the face of social and educational problems which is so typical of their environmental conditions.   The intention, of course, is not to create an uncontrolled stressful psychological situation, but rather to arrive at an objective analysis of the components of the educational environment.

(b)   The second objective was to clarify the present and prior educational characteristics of each family, and the parents' educational style.   Our technique was suggested by the theory of the T.A.T. (Thematic Apperception Test).

We showed the parents slides of relevant educational situations and invited them
to tell us what these suggested to them.   From the parents' replies we found
particular content likely to lead to atypical educational behaviour.   The
technique ensures that the parents do not become dependent on the research worker,
whose job is to help them to discover for themselves the characteristics of the
educational environment which surrounds the child.

(c)   The third objective tended to alleviate the lack of imagination of the
subjects and the effects of their limited cultural capacity.   Once the first two
objectives were attained, the parents requested our help by asking the question:
'What should we do to encourage our children's development?'   This is when we
gave the parents the pamphlet of educational activities, which suggested clearly
defined activities, each with a particular purpose.

(d)   The fourth objective also took the parents' limited education into account,
and answered the question: 'How should the psychological and educational information be communicated so that the adult does not continue to be dependent upon
the research worker?'   To convey to parents some important ideas on child development in terms comprehensible to them, we made use of strip cartoons with
supporting captions written at the reading ability level of the parents.

3.   An Approach to Psycho-linguistic Interaction in the Family
(Analysis of the corpus and comparative study of linguistic structures)

The general object of this part of the research was concerned, firstly, with the
comparative study of the spoken language of parents from two socially contrasted
groups.   We then compared the spoken language of the parents with that of their
5 to 6 year old children.   The groups were determined by socio-economic and
cultural parameters.

The comparative analysis of the different aspects of the speech of parents and
children depends on the stimulation of conversation both from parents and from
children.   The stimulus consisted of a series of 6 pictures which have to be
described.   This procedure, though restrictive, leaves the subject free to talk
in his own way and provokes him to use his linguistic resources to the full.

Here, five questions arise:
- Is there a link between the level of socio-economic and cultural disadvantage
  of the family and the language of the parents and of their children?
- Is there a positive and significant relation between the language of the
  parents and that of their children?
- If so, is it possible to reduce the linguistic handicap of deprived parents
  and children?
- If this is so, which aspects of the language would best respond to therapy?
- At which level - active vocabulary or correct syntax - is the link most
  significant?

4.   Stimulation of Parent-Child Linguistic Interactions in a Deprived
   Environment   (Report No.5)

Previous research has shown the decisive influence of the socio-cultural environment on the child's acquisition of language.   When we had completed our study
of this literature, we carried out an initial series of observations of children
in a kindergarten in Quaregnon.   This was an empirical probe into the linguistic
relationship between parents and children, and an attempt to improve the parents'

speech with the help of picture books read to the children.

The next step was to set up an experiment in two deprived districts in another village of the Borinage to develop and test a programme to stimulate parent-child linguistic interactions.   The originality of this attempt lay in the fact that the investigations were carried out entirely in the family setting.   We had four objectives:

- to help parents really to talk with the children during the reading of educational books;

- to practise the parents in reading and commenting on pictures by providing them with correct linguistic models;

- to suggest to parents educational situations which stimulate talk;

- to introduce the families to our educational brochures as cultural tools.

The results of the experiment were:

- the programme developed in the family setting raised the linguistic level of the parents;

- the child benefits indirectly from our intervention with its parents.   The effect of this was to enrich the spoken language and to raise the level of verbal intelligence;

- meetings with parents preparatory to the experiment motivated them and made it possible for them to get to know and accept us;

- a new audio-visual method and carefully produced educational pamphlets allowed us to conduct a successful programme in the families;

- an evaluation of the effectiveness of the intervention led us to think that the programme did not significantly modify the speech of the parents, but that it enabled the child to make appreciable gains in vocabulary and verbal intelligence;

- from the data collected in a complementary study of the speech of deprived parents and children, it was possible to establish a relationship between the cultural components of personality and the complexity of semantic and syntactical development.

5.   Comparing the Evaluation of two Training Programmes in Spatial Relations
     (Report No.6)

A number of findings emphasize the strong association (as well as the frequency) between success or failure in learning basic subjects and a child's capacity for spatial organisation.   The present experiment falls into the category of school activities intended to promote the acquisition of spatial concepts, and to favour the maturation of conceptualisation.

The project took place in the communes of Frameries, Flénu and Quaregnon. Seventy-two children between the ages of five and six made up the control and experimental groups.   From these children, two groups, each of 16 pupils (from contrasting social backgrounds) were given a specific programme of training in spatial organisation.   The first was mainly based on a programmed learning approach with set exercises.   It was made up of a group of pre-reading and writing activities.   It included rhythmic exercises and an ordered series of activities concerned with the structuring of space and time.   The second programme emphasised motivating first-hand experience.   It included physical exercises, the manipulation of objects and activities in both two and three dimensions.

This experiment was based on the stages of development described by Piaget. The main objectives were as follows:

- to work out and test two training programmes concerned with spatial organisation; the one using formal set tasks, the other stimulating personal expression and experimentation in the child.

- to conduct a comparative study of the changes brought about as a result of applying the two programmes to two matched samples.

- to observe the effectiveness of each programme with deprived children on the one hand, and privileged children on the other.

For the summative evaluation, the following objective tests were used:

- traditional tests for matching the samples and for the assessment of the impact of the intervention (Leiter, Terman, Maistriaux)

- tests taken from the work of Piaget, which aim to evaluate the stages of spatial conceptualisation (topographical sites, linear projection, geometrical shapes)

- specific tests (Kohs' cubes, Chassagny's squares, Borel's pattern of differently oriented signs).

It is clear from the experiment that the 'motivation' programme principally allows disadvantaged children to improve their non-verbal intelligence scores. The 'systematic' programme also enables these children to improve their non-verbal intelligence, but, in addition, it improves their conceptualisation of spatial relations. In the case of the privileged child, the application of either programme mainly develops the conceptualisation of spatial relations.

Specimen pages from the report on parents' educational attitudes (Report No.4)

19.

2. <u>The Fun of Climbing</u>

Reproduction of the
slide shown to the
parents.

At this age, the child is discovering his physical strength,
his potential. He is proud of his performance. He loves
to climb, to balance, etc. The acquisition of self-confidence
and the mastering of these actions and movements is dependent
upon an adult to make them possible.

<u>Illustration and comments by the mothers</u>

"C'est dangereux"

<u>Mrs. B., 35 years old, 2 children</u>

'Climbing walls... Here, our
garden fence is useless. The
child can climb over it. I let
him do it but often he falls...
it's no use always shouting "take
care" without explaining to him
why it's dangerous.'

20.

'Accidents'

<u>Mrs. Br., 36 years old, 2 children</u>

'Climbing walls... I wouldn't want
Cathy climbing... things happen...
you could get hurt...'

'They are developing'

<u>Mrs. D., 43 years old, 3 children</u>

'He climbs walls... it's more
dangerous, but it helps children
develop, gives their muscles
something to do... it's like
gym... it's dangerous.'

<u>Mrs. G., 31 years old, 4 children</u>

'Just look what happens when you've
got a wall... it makes them curious,
a wall, they always want to know
what's on the other side... they
don't need to have a wall to climb,
just take a look at my furniture...
at the back of us there's a low wall.
Even to watch T.V. they sometimes
climb onto a chair to sit on the
table... at the fun-fair they
wanted to climb the greasy pole...
I was just like them at their age..
here at home all the furniture's
ruined...'

Specimen pages from the programme for spatial organisation (Report No.6)

13.

6. PRESENTATION OF THE MOTIVATION PROGRAMME

A. The educational equipment

Here we have a miniature house from which the outside walls have been removed, so that the four rooms are easily accessible to the child. The child is given some miniature furniture to play with, which will help him to assimilate spatial concepts through play activities.

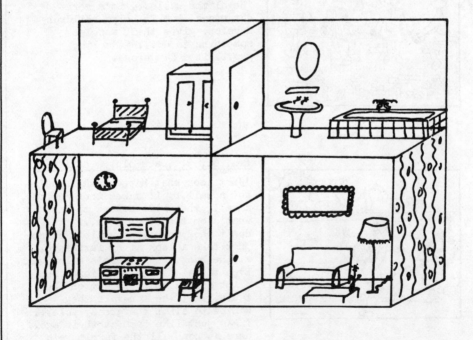

14.

Spatial concepts to be developed

The concepts considered are taken from specialized studies as
well as from several objective tests which aim to enable the
children aged four to six to grasp spatial concepts.

1. big - small
    high - low

2. up - down

3. left - right

4. in front - behind

5. far - near
    between - next to

6. above - below
    on - under

7. in - out

8. inside - outside

9. middle - side - around

10. long - short
    narrow - wide

4 Phase Three: Learning to Cooperate

The Cooperative of Educational Activities (Reports No.7 and No.8)

1. Sharing the Educational Role

The act of teaching is no longer the sole responsibility of the teacher.   The
parents are, to an equal extent, active agents in the educational process.   They
should be enabled to collaborate in the work of the project.

The creation of a cooperative of educational activities as we have seen gives
practical form to the notion of shared educational roles.   Activities aimed at
.specific learning were devised as much by the parents as by the professional
educators.

Educationalists and research workers analysed the activities from the viewpoint of
mastery learning, and thus associated formative evaluation with the empirical
contribution of both parents and teachers.

Each activity or teaching unit was described and set out in its five component
parts: the educational context, the instructions, the educational aim, the
required mental activity and the criterion of success.

The activities which had been analysed in this way were then put to the parents and
to the professional teachers who, either in groups or individually, made a critical
analysis of them after having tested and evaluated the programme.

2. Making Use of the Activities

The educational tools thus developed met the needs and motivations of the children
and the adults.   The activities could be used in a variety of settings: the
classroom, at home: and by different people: professional teachers, parents or
older children (monitorat).

The following diagram illustrates these different aspects:

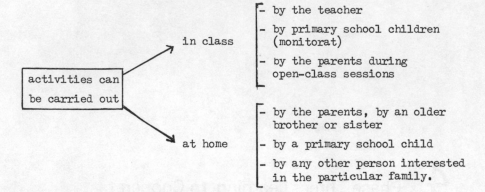

activities can
be carried out

in class
- by the teacher
- by primary school children (monitorat)
- by the parents during open-class sessions

at home
- by the parents, by an older brother or sister
- by a primary school child
- by any other person interested in the particular family.

3. The Objectives of the Cooperation

Thanks to the cooperation between school and family, the school was no longer an isolated institution. The process of training or education was extended into the community at large. Parents and professional teachers each played a part as educators whatever the material resources available either at home or in the school. The cooperative was run as much by parents as by teachers or other educational specialists, in order to:

- stimulate cooperative relationships between school and community;

- make adults aware of children's need to experiment and to express themselves;

- establish secure and supportive interpersonal relationships between children and adults;

- teach adults how to observe the activities of children and to analyse the educational environment of the community.

To set up cooperative of educational activities is not in itself sufficient. It must be supported and helped to develop by giving it specific direction. This is where the role of the educational specialist proved to be important. Every week he visited the families taking part in the experiment:

- to find out what problems were met with in the course of the activities carried out during the previous week;

- to suggest and explain new activities;

- by means of discussions and special techniques, to assess the educational climate of the family and any obstacles to the realisation of programme objectives.

4. Training the Parents

The educational specialist is also responsible for training the parents and for providing them with information. This makes it essential for him to be fully acquainted with the educational background of the families. Video tapes were shot in the home and used to show mother and child in educationally significant situations. These video tapes were played back in a room (often a classroom) where the local parents met together. During the discussion sessions which followed, the group leader used a method which allowed parents to discover for themselves the validity of the phrase 'the parents teach the parents'. They learned by themselves to identify educational behaviours of which they had hitherto been unconscious.

With these films as a starting point, further new activities were discussed.
The parents described their situations and compared their ways of dealing with
them.   Educational problems cropped up and the teacher actively participated in
the discussion.   Thus he too was initiated into a new role, that of group
leader and family counsellor in communicating his views to the parents.   From
that time onwards, he no longer worked with the child uniquely, but also with the
parents, thus achieving a real educational cohesiveness and coherence around the
child.

5. Personalization of the Project

With a series of activities at his disposal, it was possible for a teacher to
work out an individualised programme of stimulation.   In fact, the moment a
difficulty, confusion or weakness was noticed in a child's learning, the teacher
could make a rapid diagnosis and then propose alternative activities directly
adapted to the particular weakness.   If a child had problems mastering spatial
concepts such as 'far', 'above', the teacher could regroup the activities in this
section and present them so as to promote transfer and to consolidate the related
masteries.

In addition, he could generate a number of activities exemplifying the concept.
In other words, starting from the objective which gave the child difficulty, the
teacher could create new exercises to learn and practise it.

6. The Aims and Validity of the Project

This is a programme concerned with innovation in compensatory strategies.   Two
fundamental questions about the aims and validity of the educational action are
made clear and affirmed.   In fact, we can state that an educational act is only
valid in so far as it actually brings about the kind of change desired.   It
was therefore necessary, initially, to describe the objectives to be attained
and to determine the levels of mastery.   Once this is done, we can find out what,
as a result of our action, a child knows and what he can do.   We shall also know
what he has not been able to assimilate.   We may suppose that by such a method
parents would no longer have to wait for an end-of-term or end-of-year day of
judgement imposed by the school system to gain a clear idea of their child's
possibilities.

The long-term aim of the educational act is to provide the child with learning
methods and subject matter most likely to promote increased awareness and understanding of the cultural, social, economic and political environments.   In the
shorter term, the educational aims depend for their realisation upon the level
of success in the basic techniques of learning.

7. The Use of 'Monitors'

In the pre-school classes, we suggested a monitorial system (monitorat).
Pupils attending primary school took part in the activity sessions.   Each pre-
school child thus had his own monitor who suggested things the child might like
to learn, and observed the child's behaviour.

A new type of relationship was established between younger and older children.
The communal educational climate which developed seemed to encourage them to
pay greater attention to their work.   A more active and involved participation
on everyone's part was clearly evident.   This communal work builds up the self-
image both of the older and of the younger child.   The older children discover,
among other things, a new style of social relationships, greater self-confidence,
a preparation for their eventual role as parents.   The younger children reap

other benefits: more individualised teaching, more direct help, a language more
akin to their own, more personal educational help.

8. Towards More Suitable Learning Methods

The use of the series of activities had two advantages. On the one hand, the
educator, whether parent or a professional, had available a means of establishing
a learning scale and of presenting the child speedily with a range of specific
activities whenever any weakness or problem presented itself. On the other
hand, when the child had completed the series of play-activities, the educator
could feel sure that the child's intellectual capacities had been exercised in
different ways, the quantitative and qualitative importance of which was
determined according to the distribution of mental activities brought into play.

Each one of the activities in the series presented to the educator an example
which could be copied or adapted according to the difficulties and the interests
of the child and the amount of time the adult had available. In such circumstances, the educator was able to provide the kinds of activity with which the
child had experienced the greatest difficulty. In other words, effective and
efficient handling of the learning process enabled the educator to use his or
her competence in the areas decided in advance. Consequently we can suppose
that the educator will be in a position to give help where it is most needed.
We note that in this context the idea of equal chances to learn incorporates
the notion of equal chances to succeed. This advantage makes it possible to
recognise and offer each and every child the right to acquire fundamental skills
and knowledge. Thus, technology aside, it is possible to initiate an educational process which diminishes the impact of social determinants on the quality
of the learning process.

Specimen page from booklet 1 of the bank of activities (Report No.7)

1Z.

DMI – Visual language

<u>Instructions</u>

Say: "This picture is not complete.
      Would you like to finish it?"

<u>Aim</u>:   The child must be able to express himself visually
        (in this case by completing the rough sketch)

<u>Criterion of attainment</u>:   The completed drawing should
                              make sense.

Pass

Fail

Specimen page from booklet 2 of the bank of activities (Report No.7)

NMS – Spoken language

Instructions

Say: "Tell the two stories shown in these pictures."

Aim: To translate into spoken language a story
  expressed visually.

Criterion of attainment: The stories the child tells
  must express the same ideas as the pictures.

Pass

Fail

Specimen page from booklet 8 of the bank of activities (Report No.8)

MMU – Tactile memory   148.

Instructions

Say: "I am putting a duster, a newspaper and a box on the table.
When you touch them with your finger you will feel the cloth,
the paper and the wood. I'm going to cover your eyes and
change the position of the objects. Can you say which is
which now?"

Aim: 1) To be aware of the tactile sensations produced by different
materials (in this case, cloth, paper, wood)

Criterion of attainment: Recognising by touch alone the three
materials presented.

Pass

Fail

5 Conclusions and New Perspectives

The findings of the 5-year action research project in the Borinage fall into three distinct categories concerning:

a) the school as an institution

b) the family

c) the local community

1. The School as an Institution: the Pre-school

1.1 The existing system: some observations

(1) Because of its hierarchical and vertical structure, the pre-school maintains or even creates:

- an educational environment which is closed to most innovation

- relationships of dependence and subordination between the teachers and the educational authorities

- teaching methods which take scarcely any account of the social and cultural differences between families.

(2) The static character of the pre-school today dulls the children's learning ability and frequently depresses the motivation of socially disfavoured children.

(3) At entry to pre-school, the intellectual capacities of children are already differentiated by the social environments from which they come.

(4) The quality of school performance shown by deprived children is linked to the ability and commitment of the teacher.

(5) The teaching methods currently to be seen in pre-school classes do not enable socially deprived children to realise their potential competence.

1.2 The action research: its results and limitations

(1) An examination of the children's average level of school performance and an analysis of the index of social disadvantage shown by their families have

established that there are great variations from school to school.   It is thus possible to determine urgent priority areas.

(2) Our final results indicate that it is possible, so far as school performance is concerned, to reduce individual differences by modifying the learning situations both at school and within the families themselves.

(3) School results are more positive when intervention is extended to the home and when parents cooperate actively in the project.

(4) The application on a class-teaching basis of compensatory programmes, whether aimed at specific skills or general enrichment, increases the differences in performance between social groups.

(5) Apart from the direct results of specific or general compensatory programmes, most of the gains made by the children are attributable to the 'Hawthorn effect'.

(6) For children with relatively serious difficulties, a visiting (remedial) teacher can, in 85 per cent of the cases, provide effective assistance within the framework of the ordinary school.

(7) Generally speaking, there are no specific mental deficits characterising deprived children.   As a group their intellectual ability is lower than the average, and this is directly attributable to the cultural poverty of their environment.

(8) The learning units which we have developed make up the 'Cooperative of Activities':

   a) This makes it possible for professional educators to know:

   - the child's level of mastery in relation to given objectives;

   - the objectives not yet attained;

   - the learning processes to be most encouraged;

   - the variety of mental processes involved in the different learning programmes.

   b) It offers each child:

   - activities likely to favour the mastery of objectives not yet attained;

   - parallel activities related to the same objective but which take into account personal interests;

   - activities which provide practice of any mental process considered to be deficient.

(9) The act of teaching children is no longer the concern uniquely of the professional educator.

(10) At school, the task of teaching no longer devolves upon the adult alone; a child can learn with the help of another child, just as he can learn by the teaching he undertakes as a monitor.

(11) The use of a monitorial system frees the teacher from class teaching, puts a value on all members of the community, promotes relations between children and brings about a real sharing of the educational role.

(12)   As a consequence, each pre-school child has at his disposal a monitor older than himself who suggests activities, keeps an eye on his learning, takes part in his development.   This learning team is based freely on a simple mutual liking.

(13)   Effective educational cooperation is quickly established among most pupils.

(14)   It is easier for a child to model himself on other children than on a teacher who is older and more distant.

(15)   By giving pupils responsibility for one another, an active group response develops in the school, and this extends into the neighbourhood and may reach the whole community.

(16)   The monitor has to find ways to make learning easier for his team mate. When in his turn he is a pupil, he will find it easier to find a way of learning for himself.

(17)   Thus a monitorial system helps the child to learn by initiating him into the role of a teacher.

(18)   The cooperation thus brought about counteracts the rigid and hierarchical structure of the school.   It develops a sense of active mutual support inside the school community.

1.3   Future prospects

(1)   The community school must replace any school which serves the needs of a dominant minority.

(2)   The system of values of the school should reduce selection and élitism.

(3)   It is urgent to provide for and organise the in-service training of pre-school teachers.

(4)   Fundamental learning problems must be discovered very early, and certainly at the time of entry to the pre-school.

2.   The Home Environment

2.1   The present situation: findings

(1)   Parents are nowhere taught to be parents.

(2)   In the long term the social and economic environment of children account more for the differences in their success at school than do the resources or any action undertaken by the school.

(3)   In the case of immigrant workers, seven out of every ten families are socially deprived.

(4)   Eighty per cent of the parents are aware of the importance of the educational role they are called on to play.

2.2   The action research: its results and limitations

(1)   If a compensatory education programme is to have long term effect, it must include the participation of the community.

(2)   Eighty per cent of those parents who are aware of the importance of the educational role they have to play, wish to participate in the educational project at home.

(3)   On the basis of social background, the families taking part in the experiment are distributed as follows:

- well-to-do   : 9 out of 10 families

- moderately well off : 8 out of 10 families

- poor or very poor   : 7 out of 10 families

(4)   Children of foreign origin whose grandparents immigrated immediately after the 1940-45 war, achieve levels similar to those of Belgian children.

(5)   Foreign children whose parents immigrated to our country in recent years experience difficulty in integrating into the school; this is more marked in the case of children whose fathers are unskilled manual workers.

(6)   The degree of involvement of parents who agree to take part in the experiment is independent of their socio-economic level.

(7)   Vacation periods must be used profitably.   Some children between the ages of 3 and 6 years develop more when they are at home than during the time spent at school.

(8)   The educational means created by the project contribute effectively to increasing equal chances in education.

2.3   Future prospects

(1)   Any prospect of educational change depends on the parents' awareness of the need for it and on their cooperation.

(2)   The time when parental education meant 'why should we do anything?' is over; it must give way to 'how can we help?'

(3)   Introductory discussion sessions related to the education of young children must be organised to make it possible for adolescents and adults alike to participate substantially in ensuring the success of an educational project.

(4)   In socially deprived environments, information for parents about the education of their children must be practical, and must be expressed in simple, explicit language.

(5)   The methodological basis of adult education must concentrate on participation and cooperation.

3.   The Community

3.1   The present situation: findings

(1)   The school on its own cannot hope to overcome the effects of economic and political problems.

(2) Those politically responsible for the development and the execution of compensatory programmes in socially deprived communities show little more than a merely passive agreement that they should be carried out in homes and schools.

(3) Cooperation between organisations concerned with counteracting the effects of social deprivation (Child Guidance Clinics, Committees for the protection of the Youth, Committees for public assistance, etc.) is at present practically non-existent.

(4) The inadequacy of traditional teaching methods, with regard to family-school relations, is patently obvious.

3.2 The action research: its results and limitations

(1) Cooperation in school activities demonstrates that when parents and teachers share the educational role, this contributes to breaking down the formal structure of the school and to improving the educational influence of the parents.

(2) Because of the activities 'bank', children, parents, teachers and researchers collaborate and cooperate in the same educational enterprise.

(3) The quality of the parent-teacher relationship is linked to the degree of involvement and professional satisfaction shown and experienced by the teacher.

(4) The cooperative work which came about in the course of the development of teaching aids such as pamphlets containing activities, creates a bond of trust and facilitates exchanges between the parents, the teachers and the research project team.

(5) The teaching aids used during the meetings enable the parents to communicate to us their worries related to educational matters, thus providing the pre-school teachers with interesting information about the children.

3.3 Future prospects

(1) Educational responsibility for the child at all stages in his development is the concern of everyone.

(2) In their capacity as active agents in the educational process, parents and teachers must be put in a position to undertake an educational project and make it succeed.

(3) It is possible for the kindergarten to become an educational centre where parents and young people can have recent developments in education explained to them, and where they can be introduced to the use of educational techniques.

(4) The monitorial system, to have optimal effectiveness, must extend to the whole community, in which each individual would be both learner and teacher.

(5) Parents of foreign nationality who are not too familiar with the French language must be given particular attention; the technique of the monitorial system used in the home promotes both the integration of the children into the school environment and that of the parents into the community.

(6)   Educational reform cannot replace social reform.   But does the 'action
      research project' we have described not pave the way for both?

6 Recent Innovations and Developments

Since drafting our final report in 1976, a number of projects with objectives similar to those of our action research have been started in this region, and many emphasize the need for more effective measures to be taken in deprived socio-cultural environments.

The fields of operation correspond to those of our previous research, namely:

- the school
- the family
- the local community

1. Innovations involving the School

1.1   In a campaign lasting three years the Belgian Ministry of Education compiled and distributed an important series of guides dealing with pre-school education. The titles of these reflect a growing interest in the inter-university research carried out by the four Belgian research teams.   The titles are:

- Early Childhood Care and Education of Children aged 18 months to 7 years

- Language

- Rhythmical and musical education

- Mathematical exercises

- Physical education

A brief analysis of these guides can be found in an article published in 1977 in the 'Revue internationale des sciences de l'éducation' (1).

1.2 The development of the remedial class system over the past 5 years makes it possible for underprivileged children attending primary school to overcome the most serious deficiencies which check or impede their school adjustment.   Most remedial class teachers pay particular attention to beginners whose basic skills are inadequately developed for the first stages of primary school.   A large number of the children who attend these classes comes from a deprived social environment (2).

1.3 More recently, an attempt has been made to improve the transition from pre-school to primary school in several schools from each of the three educational systems in Belgium (state schools, direct grant schools and denominational schools).   The purpose of this project is to encourage each child to become aware of his own potential, and to ensure that he is able to work successfully. The experiment involves children between the ages of 5 and 8 in the final year of pre-school and in the first two years of primary school.   In theory, this experiment should make it possible for each child to make an uninterrupted transition from one stage of development to another, and to consolidate the basic learning processes characteristic of the first two years of primary school.

Details of the Belgian attempt to introduce innovations into the school curricula for 5 to 8 year old children were presented at the 5th Congress of the AIPELF (3) in Geneva, in 1977; more specific information can be found in the Nov.-Dec.1977 issue of the magazine 'L'école Belge' (4).

1.4 In 1976 a teachers' training syllabus for both pre-school and primary school levels was developed.

Under the heading 'Sociology of Education' several objectives deal with the interpersonal aspect of the educational process, the need for educational and social awareness and the analysis of educational problems.   This document is written to enable future teachers to become more aware of the problems of children from deprived environments.

1.5 The 'Civics' (or 'Ethics') syllabus in the State secondary educational system (document 315/91-1976) introduces an approach to the adolescent's social commitment to group activities.   It advocates that they should be motivated by confronting real problems of ethics 'in action'.   It favours active social participation in a cooperative and supportive atmosphere.

1.6   A recent innovative secondary school syllabus (document 315/57-1976) includes a section on family education.   Its principal objective is to 'make pupils aware of their responsibility as future parents and of the vital role played in the family by both father and mother in a child's physical, social, intellectual and emotional development'.   The teaching guide states that 'these concepts should be put forward to prepare future parents to deal with the practical problems of child health and education.   Active methods and group activities should be incorporated as often as possible in the teaching process to make the lessons more effective and realistic.'

The monitorial system developed in Mons by the Bernard van Leer Foundation research team closely resembles this approach to secondary education.

1.7 Further examples of similar projects developed on other educational levels, or within other Belgian educational systems, are still in progress.   Without making an exhaustive list, it can be said that the publications, circulars and programmes published by different academic organisations in Belgium between 1975 and 1978 point to a vast educational movement to improve the social and educational opportunities of deprived children, as well as education within the family generally.

2. Innovations involving the Family

2.1   The relevance of the objectives put forward by the Mons team, namely promotion of family awareness and participation, was confirmed in October 1977 by experts at a conference organised by the Council of Europe (5).   They opted for a general statement on pre-school education, in which the importance of the educational role of the family is clearly expressed: 'All situations, whether these be at home, at school, or elsewhere in the community, offer the pre-school

child many opportunities for learning, and all adults involved with children,
but more especially parents, play a decisive role in the child's development.'
In the course of teacher training, the importance of the role of the family, the
community and the school on the child's development should be impressed upon
students; they should be encouraged to regard their contact with parents as one
of cooperation.   Throughout the duration of pre- and primary school education,
it is important that practical measures be taken to promote the interest and
participation of parents in school activities, and teachers should be encouraged
to take a more active part in the life of the community.   In order to reduce the
differences between children, special attention should be given to those who are
educationally underprivileged.   Research can play an important part in stimulating the development of pre- and primary school education.

2.2   Eminent local educational psychologists, such as F. Hotyat, have often
pointed out the advantages to be gained from a more effective collaboration
between the school and the family (6).

2.3   J.P. Pourtois, in his Doctoral thesis (7) entitled 'How Mothers Teach
Their 5 and 6 year Olds' (October 1976) analyses different factors which
influence the child's development and its adjustment to school.   Four of his
important findings show that:

(i)   The quality of a child's development accounts for 74.47 per cent of the
        variation observed in academic achievement.

(ii)   The family accounts for 70.63 per cent of the quality of the child's
        development, through his behavioural patterns, his attitudes, his
        personality traits and intelligence and the socio-economic group from
        which he comes.

(iii)   Furthermore, the family alone accounts for 13.63 per cent of the
        variation observed in academic achievement.

(iv)   Consequently, it is possible to predict up to 88 per cent of the variation
        in academic achievement, with the help of prior knowledge of the quality
        of the child's development, and the characteristics of the family.

2.4   The Department of Educational Research continues to receive requests for
intervention and orders for pamphlets relating to family education.

3.   Innovations involving Local and Regional Organisations

3.1   The guides, which include more than 350 educational activities, are
particularly valuable for governing bodies and teaching staff in special schools,
who have frequently to take individualised learning tasks into consideration.
Our techniques are widely used in seven of the eight types of special education
defined by Belgian law. (The exception being severe mental retardation - type 2).

3.2   Child Guidance Centres, which support the educational projects carried out
in remedial classes and innovation experiments for the 5-8 year olds, have
recommended our guides to teachers involved in these new projects.

3.3   Experiments using the 'monitorial system', which involves the active
participation of vocational training school pupils of 14 to 16 years of age in
the education of 5-7 year old children, were carried out successfully during the
year 1976-1977.

3.4   The members of the DPSR have on many occasions set out the objectives and
methods of their action research at meetings organised by the Parent Teacher

Association (PTA).

3.5   In 1976 and 1977, various PTA's helped us to bring our work to the attention of a wider public by printing articles in their bulletins and periodicals.

3.6   Information concerned with the aims of family education and the analysis of techniques likely to improve it, forms an integral part of the education of students reading for a degree in Educational Psychology at the University of Mons.

REFERENCES

(1)   Burion, J.   Bilan d'une série d'innovations contrôlées en faveur d'enfants socio-culturellement handicapés.   Revue internationalle des sciences de l'éducation, 1-2, June 1977.

(2)   Detiège, L.   L'expérience des classes d'adaptation.   Revue P.M.S. No.3, Nov. 1975.

(3)   Burion, J.   Un essai belge de rénovation des apprentissages scolaires entre 5 et 8 ans.   5th Congrès de l'Association Internationale de Pédagogie Expérimentale de Langue Française, Genève, 1977

(4)   Burion, J.   Rattrapage ou étalement progressif de l'apprentissage de la lecture.   L'Ecole Belge, Nov-Dec. 1977.

(5)   Conseil de l'Europe.   CCC/EGT(17) 42 Strasbourg 25-26 October 1977.

(6)   Divers.   Au service de l'éducation : F. Hotyat.   Paris, Bruxelles, Nathan Labor, 1976.

(7)   Pourtois, J.P.   Comment les mères enseignent à leur enfant âgé de 5 à 6 ans. Doctoral thesis.   Mons, State University, 1976.   (to be published, P.U.F. Paris)

Appendix

List of the Analytical Reports Relating to the Different Stages in the Action Research Project

Phase One: Arousing Awareness

1. Education préscolairo d'cnfants socialement desavantages (203 p.)

2. Essai d'aide psycho-pédagogique aux families socialement défavorisées (80 p.)

3. Les droits de l'enfant a l'éducation (121 p.)

Phase Two: Learning to Participate

4. Pratiques éducatives, relation d'aide psycho-pédagogique et personnalité des parents (71 p.)

5. Interactions verbales parents-enfants (142 p.)

6. Organisation spatiale à l'école maternelle (70 p.)

Phase Three: Learning to Cooperate

7. Coopérative d'activités éducatives, vol.1 (165 p.)
    Langage graphique - langage oral - langage gestuel -
    déchiffrement de symboles - activités logico-mathématiques

8. Coopérative d'activités éducatives, vol.2 (215 p.)
    Mémoire visuelle - mémoire auditive - mémoire tactile -
    organisation spatiale - organisation temporelle - activités de
    motricité générale - activités de motricité fine - activités
    visuelles - activités auditives - activités tactiles -
    troubles d'articulation - troubles du langage - troubles de la
    fonction symbolique.

Part 5

General Conclusions

General Conclusions

In the nature-nurture controversy there is no current consensus. Nevertheless, it is probable that innate endowment sets limits to the power of education; and it is quite certain that differences of all kinds abound. In the present group of studies they appeared in individual development, in the attitudes and in the practice of parents and teachers, and in the ways in which institutions were used by their clients. Hence we have to take account of the variabilities of behaviour in their relation to the structures and rhythms of development, to how these are used and expressed on the one hand and, on the other, of the psycho-social and institutional contexts in which they evolve. Within this total field of forces, as it were, the stimulation provided by the environment is the one possible point of entry as a lever for change. The power of the environment to produce differences is real. And this fact underscores the urgency of further research and of the appropriate economic, psycho-social, political and educational measures.

In their work, the four university research teams tried to break away from earlier conceptual and methodological naiveties by:

- clarifying the independent socio-economic and cultural variables;

- identifying the intervening variables (educational attitudes, personality characteristics and so on);

- demonstrating that these intervening variables differ in their effects according to developmental levels or stages of the pre-school or primary school career;

- establishing the functional interdependence between behaviour and the precise school context, between learning styles and styles of teaching.

All the teams emphasised that change presupposes that teachers, parents and administrators must become fully aware of the problem and cooperate in its solution.

1. Results

The work done shows:

1.1 Psychological development

Between the tenth and twenty-first month of life the development of children is not directly related to the socio-economic and cultural level of the parents.

None of the indices used indicates marked differences between children from favoured or unfavoured environments. On the other hand, maternal styles are related to socio-economic and cultural factors and configurations of maternal attitudes can be distinguished which are strongly linked to levels of development above or below average, harmonious or inharmonious.

The longitudinal study shows that from two or three years of age, a gap opens which is related to socio-economic and socio-cultural factors. The difference does not seem, to any significant degree, to be an artefact of the tests used. At this age, the child's development seems to reflect family attitudes which had been diagnosed early on. Attitudes which imply respect for the child, acceptance of and empathy for him, are more favourable to growth in the medium term than are those which could be called exigent and stress training for specific performance, attitudes which, in younger children, do produce a transitory acceleration.

In a general sense, among socially deprived children at five years, there are no specific deficits in cognitive structures. Nevertheless their generally lower level of cognitive functioning does seem to be associated with the cultural characteristics of their school and home environments.

1.2 Institutions and individuals

Authoritarian, hierarchical and bureaucratic structures impede psychological involvement and the acceptance of personal responsibility for the job. The quality of relationships among parents, teachers and children tends to reflect the degree of the teachers' professional satisfaction. Genuine discussion and free exchange of experience is the basis of real participation, acceptance of responsibility and true insight into problems and possible solutions. With this in mind, the research workers sought cooperation with teachers, a sharing of their knowledge, and tried to evoke an awareness of the aims and possibilities of interaction.

1.3 The measures taken

What takes place within the family before the child goes to school seems critical to its subsequent general development and to educational progress. It is at this age that the child builds up its self image, a crucial stage determining his psychological and psycho-social levels as well as his fundamental security.

Parents are active agents of education. The 'profession' of parenthood is not learned anywhere, yet parenting is one of the most important tasks facing society today.

Short-term general or specific stimulation programmes have only short-term results. They do not prevent social disadvantage interfering with school learning.

Frontal type programmes, whether they attempt general enrichment or specific compensatory teaching, are more likely to increase differences in the achievement of children from different social groups. Nevertheless, many children at risk at the very beginning of school can be greatly helped by a programme of general stimulation, coupled with specific compensatory activities and group work. Such programmes lose much of their effect if they are not continued in the primary school.

Each team found some idiosyncracies in the patterns of variation observed, and sometimes a clear reduction in differences, both of development and of specific learned skills. This brings up the problem of the objectives and norms on which evaluation is based.

On one hand, the maximum number of children should be helped to achieve the greatest number of those objectives considered essential, that is one aims to homogenise results with reference to basic criteria. On the other hand, each child must be given the chance to develop fully, through a greater differentiation of educational practices.

2. Policy Suggestions

The results achieved hitherto suggest the following recommendations for educational policy.

2.1 Stimulation strategies

The family, crèche, the nursery and primary school are the best and most obvious places for general educational action to stimulate children's creativity and spontaneity. Structured strategies and specific exercises should always be subordinated to a general strategy which neglects neither personality development, the role of the self-image nor the impact of social relationships. The interplay of the factors involved (persons, strategies, institutions, etc.) will provide the context determining any educational intervention. Each team, in its own way, stressed the importance of relationships in education which deeply affect how and if a child acquires knowledge and skill. A positive learning environment is marked by attitudes of acceptance, by the way it takes into account and concentrates on the child's own experiences and culture, and by the positive expectations held about his capacities.

2.2 Teacher training

Communication between all parties involved in the educational process should be promoted and at all levels. One of the most essential elements in teacher training is the emphasis on the social and personal dimensions of educational relationships. Concentration on content, on instructional techniques, frequently blinds teachers to the child itself. Teacher training should be thought out afresh. New teaching methods should take into account recent work in the sciences of education, in formulating objectives and in determining and evaluating methods.

2.3 Further research

Current developmental and learning theory cannot by itself prescribe the objectives and techniques of differentiated teaching. It is not the place of the research worker or the politician to prescribe any particular model for intervention. Any such model should arise from practical cooperation on the job between those most nearly involved: parents, teachers, research workers and administrators. The research focuses action and action validates research; and strategic decisions should be based on this interaction.

Action research should also be integrated with fundamental research. Thus, for example, we come to see the importance of longitudinal studies of the same children from different social backgrounds, and which followed them through the first years of life into their nursery and primary schools. Nor should we neglect, in any global scheme, the importance of adolescence.

The critical phases of the action research cannot be hurried if we are to gain conclusions which can be safely generalised. Here we are thinking notably of the setting up of adequately representative samples, continuous reconceptualisation of objectives and their practical embodiment, the processes of perfecting strategies, and methods of education and the evaluation of results.

Continuous involvement of teachers in research will make them more aware and more able themselves to choose objectives and strategies which take into account the possibilities of intervention, plans of action and evaluation.

Action research in the field of parent education would help train and prepare parents and parents-to-be for their role as educators.

2.4 Strategies for change

Strategies for change grew within each project from contacts with people who are frequently isolated in the current system. They came together to discuss and work together.   They not only developed programmes but also examined their own positions and asked questions about their own institutions.   Such a situation fostered real innovation directed at reducing inequality in education.   It began to bring about a real continuity between:

- groups of children of different ages;
- the family, school and local community through greater knowledge of the social reality experienced by children and adults;
- the various points of intervention from earliest childhood up to the beginning of compulsory schooling.

The importance of early intervention, and its essential unity and continuity through time necessitates a breaking of the present separation of educational, health and cultural policies.

The education of adults concerned is an interesting aspect and one of the ways for continuing education.

Most of these recommendations have not gone beyond the stage of good intentions. Nonetheless, it should be noted that our work has already put into practice some of the proposals for educational policy and effective innovation put forward by international organisations (1).   Ours is part of a contemporary movement in research which sprang from the failure of vast, centralised programmes and from the need for effective participation on the part of all parties involved in a reform:

- Decentralised programme development by means of action research.
- Constant feedback and revision.
- Consultation between those administratively and politically responsible and their partners in practical educational enterprise.
- Dissemination of results, not by administrative fiat in readymade packets, but by making them available for adaptation or even re-creation at the local level.
- A system of evaluation which recognises the legitimate right of all those concerned to take part in it.

The goal of these suggestions is to give everyone, in practice and not only in theory, whether an individual or a member of a social group, the right and the means to develop and to participate in changing the school and society itself.

REFERENCE

(1) Conseil de l'Europe, <u>Problèmes d'évaluation dans l'éducation préscolaire</u>.
Centre de documentation pour l'éducation en Europe, Strasbourg, 1975.

Conseil de l'Europe, <u>Compensatory education</u>.
Documentation center for education in Europe, Strasbourg, 1975.

Centre for Educational Research and Innovation, <u>Developments in Early
Childhood Education</u>. OECD/CERI, Paris, 1975.

Publications by or on behalf of the Bernard van Leer Foundation

Monographs

Early childhood education in the Caribbean: a seminar report. The Hague, 1972. Pp.56.

Early childhood education in Jamaica: a project monograph. The Hague, 1972. Pp.47.

Educating Africa's youth for rural development, by Archibald Callaway. The Hague, 1974. Pp.95.

Curriculum in early childhood education: a seminar report. The Hague, 1974. Pp.172.

Innovation in early childhood education: report of the second Caribbean seminar. The Hague, 1974. Pp.115.

The Scrowe Brigades: Alternative Education in Botswana, by Patrick van Rensburg. London, Macmillan, 1978. Pp.VI + 74.

Sustainability of change in education: Report on the First Eastern Hemisphere Seminar on Early Childhood Education. The Hague, 1978. Pp.156.

Bibliographies

Compensatory eary childhood education: a selective working bibliography. The Hague, 1971. Pp.355.

Parent involvement in early childhood education: Selected titles. The Hague, 1976. Pp.96.

Evaluation studies on early childhood education programmes: Selected titles. The Hague, 1977. Pp.128.

Bi-lingual learning in multi-racial societies: Selected titles. The Hague, 1978. Pp.321.